The Novels of Achebe and Ngugi

In the same series

Recent Commonwealth Literature (2 Vols.)
R.K. Dhawan, A.K. Srivastava and P.V. Dhamija, ed.

The Novels of Wole Soyinka
M. Rajeshwar

Indian Response to African Writing
A. Ramakrishna Rao and C.R. Visweswara Rao, ed.

South Asian Response to Chinua Achebe
Bernth Lindfors and Bala Kothandaraman, ed.

The Novels of Ayi Kwei Armah
K. Damodar Rao

Australian Literature and Indian Literature: Studies in Mutual Response
David Kerr and R.K. Dhawan, ed.

Australian Literature Today
R.K. Dhawan and David Kerr, ed.

New Zealand Literature Today
R.K. Dhawan and Walter Tonetto, ed.

A.D. Hope: Questions of Poetic Strength
Walter Tonetto

The Novels of Achebe and Ngugi

A Study in the Dialectics of Commitment

K. Indrasena Reddy

PRESTIGE

Published by
Prestige Books
New Delhi 110 008

Rs. 400
Prestige Books

ISBN: 81-85218-88-9

Phototypesetting by
Pivot Computers
Delhi 110 006
Phone 2918404

Printed at
Mehra Offset Press
Delhi 110 006

Contents

To

the memory of my father

Preface

The term 'Orature' coined by Pio Zirimu, a Ugandan linguist and literary critic, traces the oral antecedents of African literature. There has been a serious debate about the origins and the thematic concerns of African literature which is mostly concerned with the traumatic experiences of the natives consequent on the colonization of the Continent and later with neo-colonial scenario.

Achebe and Ngugi are concerned with the portrayal of the African as insiders and they have been able to erase the savage image imputed to him by the racist writers. African literature has received worldwide recognition with the award of the Nobel Prize in Literature to Wole Soyinka in 1986, and Nadine Gordimer in 1991. The award of the 1992 Nobel Prize to Derek Walcott (West Indies) and in 1993 to Toni Morrison, an Afro-American woman writer, testifies to the tremendous potentialities of the African experience and its actualization through literature.

African critics have been able to demonstrate the native origins of the African fiction tracing it to its "Oral Narrative Forms" while debunking the theory of its being derived from the "European Model." Chinweizu's *Toward the Decolonization of African Literature* is a trend-setter in this direction whereas Chidi Amuta's *The Theory of African Literature*, a monumental study in African criticism, locates the African novel in post-modernist dialectics. Achebe's *Anthills of the Savannah* returns to this oral tradition with a bang in order to grasp, reevaluate and pass on to posterity the age-old wisdom as embodied in the folk tales, folk songs, myths and legends of the land. While Achebe has been able to thoroughly indigenise the very genre of fiction through his novels, Ngugi is involved in a relentless pursuit to decolonize the African literature itself.

The present study is confined to the evaluation of Achebe's *Things Fall Apart, Arrow of God* and *Anthills of the Savannah* and Ngugi's *The River Between, A Grain of Wheat* and *Petals of Blood*. Achebe's major concern in these novels is the problem of power (political) and the struggle to contain it, whereas for Ngugi, religion and rebellion are complementary to each other. Commitment in Achebe and Ngugi meet and mix in the interplay of "Power, Struggle, Religion and Rebellion."

Acknowledgements

I am deeply indebted to Prof. Satyanarain Singh who closely monitored the present work. I wish to record my gratitude to Prof. C.L. Innes of the University of Kent (England) with whom I worked at Canterbury on this project and to Prof. Dennis Brutus, Chairperson, Black Studies Department, Pittsburgh, U.S.A., for his guidance. My sincere thanks are due to Prof. Jafar Nizam, former Vice-Chancellor, Kakatiya University, Warangal, for the sanction of short-term U.G.C Fellowship which enabled me to collect material for my work in England and America. I am grateful to Dr. K Jayashankar, Vice-Chancellor, Kakatiya University, and Prof. C.K. Kokate for the partial funding of this work as well as to the University Grants Commission, New Delhi, for the grant. My special thanks are due to Prof. Shiv K. Kumar, Prof. K. Venkatachari, Prof. Subba Rao, Mr. A. Madhusudan Reddy I.A.S., and Dr. R.K. Dhawan, for their help and guidance. I would like to acknowledge my gratitude to Prof. B. Ramakrishna Reddy, Prof. Abdur Rahman, Dr. T. Venkat Reddy and Dr. M. Janardhan Reddy for their suggestions and support. I wish to thank Dr. V. Gopal Reddy and Mr. Ramaiah, Librarian, CIEFL, Hyderabad, and his staff who helped me in several ways. Finally my sincere thanks are due to Mr. G. Srinivas and Mr. Mahesh for the technical services rendered by them in bringing out this work. My thanks are due to Prestige Books, New Delhi, for bringing out this book elegantly and expeditiously.

Eurocentricity vs. Afrocentricity

Introductory

This chapter is concerned with the emergence of African fiction and its context; it seeks to present briefly the available criticism on Achebe and Ngugi; and it also tries to discuss the nature of commitment in these two writers.

African fiction emerges as a kind of reaction to the Eurocentric version of the African portrayed in terms of "a savage" inhabiting "a dark continent." Joyce Cary's *Mister Johnson* and Conrad's *Heart of Darkness* typify this distorted African image. As late as 1963, Hugh Trevor Roper, Professor of Modern History at Oxford, observed in a television broadcast: "There is only the history of Europeans in Africa. The rest is darkness – and darkness is not a subject of history."[1] This is what the Oxford Professor of History says even after Achebe's *Things Fall Apart* (1958) appeared with a clear message as to the history of Africa well constructed in the novel. The European sensibility is either ignorant of the apparent reality around it or refuses to accept what is inconvenient.

African fiction is very much seized with the traumatic experiences the scars of which are left behind by colonialism. Like all other art-forms in Africa, African fiction has a functional value. Unlike his European counterpart who suffers from an alienated image, the African novelist is part of the mainstream of his society. African novel has been able to establish a tradition and an aesthetic of its own in a short span of time. It is in a position to debunk many schools of criticism, the school of "art for art's sake" in particular. The functional role of African fiction is committed to drawing and involving its people in a nation building activity. Achebe's and Ngugi's novels are committed to this task.

II

More than any other African writer, Achebe has received maximum critical attention. There have been a good number of full-length studies on his works. C.L. Innes's *The Devil's Own Mirror* (1990) brings out succinctly the striking similiarities in John Synge's *Playboy of the Western*

World and Achebe's *Things Fall Apart* in terms of "cultural nationalism" [2] as inspiring national movements in Ireland and Africa. In addition to these sources, every critical study devoted to African literature/fiction has invariably an essay or a chapter on Achebe's fiction. Further, numerous critical essays have been proliferating in various journals the world over delineating, and sometimes duplicating, various aspects of Achebe's fiction.

The earliest among the full-length studies on Achebe's writings, fiction in particular, are G.D. Killam's *The Novels of Chinua Achebe* (1969) and an anthology of essays: *Critical Perspectives on Chinua Achebe* (1978), edited by C. L. Innes and Bernth Lindfors.

Killam's book was revised and published in 1977 under a new title *The Writings of Chinua Achebe* so as to include a chapter each on Achebe's poetry and short stories. This study considers the heroes of his first three novels as conceived in tragic terms,

> men in varying degrees conscious of the fact that life turns out to be less manageable and less perfect than they had expected, they react to life in various ways with courage, honesty and generosity, with pessimism and cynicism – in their attempts to get through life with honour and reward. [3]

The three novels are discussed as tragedies in their own right by Killam. "This triology of novels reveals the extent to which traditional values have been turned upside down and ends in gloom and uncertainty." [4] *A Man of the People*, however, marks a change from this tragic tradition and is "more immediate in subject and more deliberately polemical in purpose." [5]

Killam's study explains at length how the traditional and well-knit society of Igboland is disrupted so that it "falls apart" under the pressure of colonial values. The major finding of this book is embodied in a statement according to which Achebe's fictional strategy is "one of implication rather than explication" leaving "much unsaid," and in this process, Achebe "achieves a suggestiveness which communicates far more than he might achieve in long passages of explicit description." [6]

Critical Perspectives on Chinua Achebe [7] has five essays each of general nature, on *Things Fall Apart* and *Arrow of God*; three on *A Man of the People* and two on *No Longer at Ease*. The Bibliography section appended to this book is very exhaustive and useful for Achebe scholars.

"The Tragic Conflict in the Novels of Chinua Achebe" by Abiola Irele seeks to reiterate and reinforce the line of argument of G.D. Killam fixing

Achebe's novels in a tragic tradition. A.G. Stock's essay "Yeats and Achebe," related to *Things Fall Apart* mainly, is very insightful and highly philosophical. It seeks to link together two great writers from different cultural backgrounds. The essay deals with the inevitable fall of civilizations with which both Yeats and Achebe are concerned in "The Second Coming" and *Things Fall Apart* respectively. The editorial and introductory observation as to the deceptive simplicity of Achebe's novels is worth recording here: "the apparent simplicity of Achebe's novels is deceptive and . . . the discerning reader may discover beneath their surface a complex and subtle interplay of values and attitudes." [8]

These two studies provide the necessary background for further exploration of Achebe's fiction. The two books look at Achebe's novels with the two important facets of the novelist in terms of anthropological/sociological background and the break-down of the age-old value systems of the Igbos in Nigeria under the influence of colonialism.

Robert Wren's *Achebe's World* published in 1980 inaugurates the second and more serious phase in Achebe's critical analysis. The book does a lot more than explicate the *Historical and Cultural Context of the Novels of Chinua Achebe* as indicated by its title. It offers incisive insights into the "apparent simplicity" of Achebe's fiction. *Achebe's World* also reinforces the main line of argument of Killam in terms of Achebe's method of "implication" and "suggestiveness."

Wren's critical analysis of Achebe's fiction takes up the most crucial and vital issue in each of Achebe's novels, focusing on the implication it has in the context of the novel concerned. Wiping out a whole village (Abame) in *Things Fall Apart* as a retaliation for the killing of a single white man; the irony involved in the formation of a Confederation of six villages of Umuaro for reasons of safety and security against the marauders from a neighbouring country in *Arrow of God*; Mr. Green's simplification of the natives' psyche and fallibility as "victims of the worst climate in the world" in *No Longer at Ease* – signify much more than what meets the eye. Each incident has an endless tale to tell. Finally, Chief Nanga's (in *A Man of the People*) unabashed methods of bribery, corruption, "violent intimidation" and murder in cold-blood in the post-independence climate – constitute an explosive situation and a potential threat to the very body politic of the nation. The book also offers vital historical, anthropological background and annotations to the novels. It also includes an exhaustive glossary of Igbo words and names which are of immense value to a non-Nigerian scholar.

C.L. Innes's *Chinua Achebe* (1990) places "a particular emphasis on Achebe's Africanization of the novel, trying to discern what elements he has used and what innovations he has made in his development as a novelist." [9] The chapter "Critic as a Novelist" on *Anthills of the Savannah* offers an excellent analysis of the novel in terms of the novelist's metamorphosis into a critic of his society in the post-independence era. Innes also discusses Achebe's use of language with reference to his innovation in narrotology.

Felicity Riddy's "Language as a Theme in *No Longer at Ease*," Bernth Lindfors's "The Palm-oil with which Achebe's Words are Taken," and Gareth Griffith's "Language and Action in the Novels of Chinua Achebe" deal with Achebe's techniques and innovations in English language. Achebe aims at fashioning out a new English with an unmistakable African flavour about it.

Modern Fiction Studies (Vol. 37, No. 3, Autumn 1991) has a special section on Achebe's fiction. Kofi Owusu's "The Politics of Interpretation: The Novels of Chinua Achebe" deals with "the use and abuse of power by those who wield it" [10]–the protagonists in Achebe's novels. Onyemaechi Udumukwu's "Achebe and the Negation of Independence" addresses itself to "Achebe's reaction against the negation of the expectations of national independence from colonial rule" [11] with reference to *A Man of the People* and *Anthills of the Savannah*; Roben Ikamegi's "Knowledge and Power, the Story and the Story-teller: Achebe's *Anthills of the Savannah*" delineates the nexus between knowledge, power and the story and the story-teller.

Charles Larson's *The Emergence of African Fiction* and Adrian Roscoe's *Mother is Gold: West African Literature* treat African literature, fiction in particular, condescendingly and from a Eurocentric point of view. Chinweizu and others in their trend-setting critical book, *Toward the Decolonization of African Literature* attack Larson's and Roscoe's nauseating theories of "Universality" and "malicious Eurocentric criticism," [12] designed to denigrate African literature. Larson in *The Emergence of African Fiction* seeks to make a mockery of the profound and "well-made" (Larson's obsession with "well-made story" in fiction is comparable with Arnold's "touch-stone" method as a critical tool) novels of Achebe – *Things Fall Apart* and *Arrow of God* and a host of other great novels – by many more African novelists. For Larson, these novels are no more than "a series of short tales strung together, or a collection of short stories tied together" or "many unrelated essays and stories." [13] Achebe assails these Eurocentric critics as "colonialist" in their intentions and sensibility.

An anthology of essays included in *South Asian Responses* to *Chinua Achebe* is probably the most recent critical work on Achebe. Mention may be made of at least three essays in this volume – namely, Supriya

Nair's "The Story and Struggle in *Anthills of the Savannah*"; "Achebe and the Indians" by Bernth Lindfors and Bala Kothandaraman's piece on Achebe's "Short Stories." The editorial comment which figures in the 'Preface' of the book seeks to sum up succinctly the relevance of the writings of Achebe in the "Third-World" context. Achebe's writings are in the nature of a challenge to the "First World Centricity." The editors maintain: "Today Achebe's art speaks not only to and for Africa but also to and for much of the rest of the 'Third World,' not least through its successful challenge of 'First World' centricity." Bernth Lindfors' essay should be an eye-opener to the Eurocentric Indian academics entrusted with the job of designing syllabi at the Indian universities.

My evaluation of Achebe's fiction in terms of power equations with reference to the degenerated values and their impact on the people and the body politic of the country is sought to be projected through the study of the three representative novels, *Things Fall Apart, Arrow of God* and *Anthills of the Savannah*. This area has not been adequately dealt with and has much scope for further exploration.

III

Like Achebe, Ngugi wa Thiong'o has also attracted critical attention from different parts of the world and there is a large body of critical writings on Ngugi's works. There is no dearth of full-length studies on Ngugi's writings. Critical essays on Ngugi in different literary, non-literary journals the world over have been proliferating. One of the earliest among the full-length studies on Ngugi is G.D. Killam's *An Introduction to the Writings of Ngugi*, published in 1980.

According to Killam, "the life in his (Ngugi's) novels is shaped by the presence of Christianity," [15] and his first novel *The River Between* was written "when he was a devout Christian." [16] Christianity is a major influence in both the colonial and neo-colonial novels of Ngugi. *A Grain of Wheat* and *Petals of Blood* abound in Biblical allusions.

'History' is yet another major influence on Ngugi's fiction. His first four novels cover a span of six decades (1920s onwards) and "draw on documented historical fact as background." [17] Both Achebe and Ngugi focus on the historical aspect in their fiction. Killam also accounts for the influence of Marx and Fanon on Ngugi's writings, *A Grain of Wheat* and *Petals of Blood* in particular. Killam observes: "It is Marx who articulates a political and economic philosophy which will suit Ngugi's conviction about post-independent Kenyan development. It is Fanon who places the thinking of Marx in the African context." [18]

Two more influences on Ngugi as cited by Killam are Lawrence and

Conrad. Killam's assessment of *A Grain of Wheat* is very thought-provoking. He says:

> *A Grain of Wheat* is not a political novel in the fullest sense. The political theme is balanced against the exploitation of human fallibility the novel offers. Ngugi's humanism, revealed by his care for his people and his understanding of what prompts them to action, dominates the novel.[19]

Killam's annotation of the names of major characters in *Petals of Blood* is very revealing:

> Munira means 'stump' and this describes his devitalized state in the novel, his inability to connect with those around him. . . . Wanja comes from "Wanjiku," the mother of the nine clans of Gikuyu land. Wanja also means 'stranger or outsider.' Karega means "he-who-refuses" (to fall in line) and remains "an archetypal non-confirmist . . . searching for a cause to the statis of anti-establishment revolutionary leader. . . . The M.P. for Ilmorg, the Hon' Nderi wa Riera means "vulture son of air." . . . Njuguna represents the 'common man.'[20]

Killam's annotation of the names of characters in *Petals of Blood* with their "allegorical associations" is striking and significant. Killam's study, thus, is more than a mere "introduction" to Ngugi's writings and is a pioneering and major contribution to the body of Ngugi's criticism.

C.B. Robson's *Ngugi wa Thiong'o*, yet another early full-length critical study on Ngugi, was published in 1979. Robson's study traces the growth and development of Ngugi as a writer whose "social, historical and political base"[21] ultimately transforms him into "a radical and revolutionary writer."[22] According to Robson, Ngugi's achievement as a writer lies in the latter's ability to go beyond "the dramatisation of history, and its interpretation" so that "he penetrates the surface details of history and draws on underlying human concerns."[23]

Robson comments on the "linear movement" in the novels of Ngugi around which he "develops various concerns"[24] underlying human relationships at the societal level with reference to a historical setting. Robson also elaborates on Ngugi's use of myth, story and symbolism for the evocation of various responses in different contexts in his novels.

Robson's assessment of *Petals of Blood* with reference to the issue of 'power' is a significant contribution to the available criticism on the novel. Quoting from Christopher Rick's "Power without Glory in Kenya" published in *The Sunday Times* (26 Jan. 1977), Robson comments on the various "aspects of power and their effect." For instance, "Munira's power of education, Karega's trade-union power, and Wanja's power over men illustrate this" [25] and finally, "money" as "power" in the context of the novel. Robson's critical study is of great value to the ever-growing body of criticism on Ngugi's writings.

David Cook and Michael Okenimpke's *Ngugi: An Exploration of His Writings* (1983) is probably the most comprehensive, balanced and insightful critical study covering all the works of Ngugi (fiction, non-fiction, drama and short stories) from every possible angle.

The authors of this study point out how and to what extent Ngugi's writings are conditioned by the abject poverty suffered by his family when he was a boy; the socio-political situation in Kenya to which Ngugi is alive perceptively in colonial and neo-colonial phases; the radical atmosphere at Leeds in 60s when he was a student there; and finally, the influence of Marx and Fanon on him in shaping his ideological position. The study also points out the autobiographical element, rather "the parallels between fact and fiction." [26]

The critical study under discussion traces out three important phases in Ngugi's writing. In the first phase, terminating with his graduate study at Makerere in 1963, Ngugi "evinces an essentially moralist-humanist outlook on human affairs." [27] *The River Between* reflects the author's mood of this phase. The middle phase of Leeds and his early teaching career represent "a period of maturing vision in which his attention is focussing upon such large ideas and events as Mau-Mau, capitalism, socialism and nationalism." [28] The essays in *Homecoming* and the novel, *A Grain of Wheat*, are the representative writings of this period. The third phase of Ngugi's writings following his detention for a year and his subsequent exile on his own from Kenya "is marked by a corrosive disillusionment with the character of social forces in independent Africa, particularly Kenya, and a bitter revulsion against the emerging African elite and middle-class." [29] *Petals of Blood* and most other non-fictional prose-writings written during this phase hold a mirror to Ngugi's transformation into a revolutionary writer.

The authors quote Ngugi's own appraisal of Achebe's *A Man of the People* wherein Ngugi is as much intrigued as Achebe himself as to the ordering of one's priorities in a situation which brooks no delay and has an immediacy about it. In his discussion of *A Man of the People*, Ngugi observes: "Which do you change first in a society, its politico-economic base (new foundations for a new house of a different nature) or the morality of individual men and women?" [30] The answer comes home to him in the decisive third stage of his writing wherein he rejects the existing social institutions and power structures left behind as a colonial legacy and recommends a socialist order in their place.

The last chapter in this book, "Literature and Society," tries to capture the mood of the novelist as discernible in all the three phases of Ngugi's writing. The authors point out that *The River Between* (of the first phase) seeks resolution for the crisis in the novel "in terms of man's enduring spiritual values." [31] In *A Grain of Wheat* of the middle phase, Ngugi's "stand on social issues becomes steadily more . . . radical, but as an artist he is still controlled by his aesthetic awareness." [32] *Petals of Blood* of the crucial third stage brings "face to face . . . the oppressors and the oppressed, the overfed and the starving, the predators and their victims," [33] and involves them in a grim battle. This study on Ngugi's writings is a very valuable and significant contribution to the body of criticism on the writer.

Emmanuel Ngara's book *Art and Ideology in the African Novel*[34] has a chapter on Ngugi's novels. This chapter maps out how Ngugi's "ideological perspective has developed from nationalist politics to revolutionary politics, from critical realism to socialist art." [34] Simon Gikandi's essay, "On Culture and the State: The Writings of Ngugi wa Thiong'o" points out how the "novelist's life and his literary products have been shaped by politics of nationalism, its initial promise and eventual failure." [35] This essay also explicates the irony of Ngugi's historical circumstances:

> the very moment he has rediscovered his individual utterance is also the moment at which he is furthest removed from the people for and about whom he writes. Branded by the state of Kenya as public enemy number one, Ngugi recently published his latest novel, *Matigari* (1986) only to have the book impounded almost immediately in the publisher's offices in Nairobi. [36]

Simon Gikandi's 'profile' on Ngugi drives home the message as to the methods of the repressive regime of Arap Moi in Kenya which seeks to 'silence' dissent from its critics by banning books considered to be subversive from its point of view.

Chidi Amuta places Ngugi in the company of great writers and thinkers like Fanon and Cabral. He says: "Taken together, the views of Fanon, Cabral and Ngugi . . . contain . . . the kernel and essential ingredients of a dialectical theory of African literature and culture." [37] This tribute to Ngugi speaks volumes about his relevance and importance as a commited contemporary writer.

I propose to discuss Achebe and Ngugi from the viewpoint of their particular perception of African reality in the context of the colonial and neo-colonial encounter and their commitment to African values against the perspective of the fast declining moral standards in public life with scant respect for work ethics and work culture in the post-independence era. Both the writers are sadly disillusioned with civilian rule (followed by a succession of military coups in Achebe's Nigeria) due to rampant corruption in the wake of insatiable greed for power, pleasure and profit, excessive indulgence in hypocrisy, intrigue, violence, manipulations and machinations in power-equations.

IV

> I believe it is impossible to write anything in Africa without some kind of commitment, some kind of message, some kind of protest . . . because there were people who thought we didn't have a past. What we were doing was to say we did – here it is. [38] Achebe

> Violence in order to change an intolerable, unjust social order is not savagery: it purifies man. Violence to protect and preserve an unjust, oppressive social order is criminal, and diminshes man. [39]
>
> Ngugi

Both Chinua Achebe and Ngugi are committed writers. The two statements quoted above by Achebe and Ngugi clarify the nature of their commitment as writers. Non-prose fiction of these writers documents their approach and attitude in relation to their societies, culture, art history, language and literature. Apart from the non-fictional prose of these writers, the later fiction of both the writers evidences such commitment in *Anthills of the Savannah* and *Petals of Blood.*

Commitment of the two writers in respect of the medium of language in their writings is drastically different from one another. Achebe is alive to the indispensability of English which has been thrust on Africa as a colonial legacy. He feels apologetic and 'guilty' that he is left with no alternatives. He says: "Is it right that a man should abandon his mother tongue for someone else's? It looks like a dreadful betrayal and produces a guilty feeling. . . . But for me there is no other choice. I have been given this language and I intend to use it." [40] Achebe slightly modifies this statement later to go on record about the "fatalistic logic of the unassailable position of English in our literature." [41] In any case, Achebe accepts this "fatalistic logic" as a challenge and has been able to thoroughly Africanize both English and the genre of fiction showing the way for younger generation of writers to emulate him as a model.

Ngugi regrets that such great writers as Achebe, Soyinka, and Kofi Awonoor should have chosen "not to revitalise the African novel . . . to create a new tradition, that of the African novel," [42] Ngugi acknowledges that his fiction also upto *A Grain of Wheat* and *Petals of Blood* belongs to this tradition of Afro-European novel. He says: "After I had written *A Grain of Wheat* I underwent a crisis. I knew whom I was writing about but whom was I writing for?" [43] He told himself not to write any longer in English as part of his commitment to write only in his native idiom so as to get across his message to the common people. His first experiment in writing and staging a play in Gikuyu *Ngaahika Ndeenda (I will marry when I want)* registered instant success. It is a critique on the government. The play was banned and Ngugi detained. However, his determination to write his future works in Gikuyu remains unshaken. He went on record to say: "I would attempt a novel in the very language which had been the basis of incarceration. I would reconnect myself not to the Afro-European novel of my previous practice but to the African novel of my new commitment." [44] The two novels he wrote later are in Gikuyu. However, these novels, *Devil on the Cross* and *Matigari* have been translated into English by himself. Ngugi feels duty bound to nurture and enrich African languages. He wrote: "We African writers are bound by our calling to do for our languages what Spenser, Milton and Shakspeare did for English; what Pushkin and Tolstoy did for Russian." [45] These statements of Ngugi are very explicit and seek to explain his stand on English vis-a-vis the languages of Africa.

Ngugi's *The River Between* (his first novel written in English) and Achebe's *Things Fall Apart* accomplish these writers' commitment to demonstrate to both the Western world and their own that Africa had a glorious past, history, traditions and culture which they could be proud of. Achebe's essay "Novelist as Teacher" is part of the writer's commitment to help his people get rid of the racial inferiority and restore their humanity to them in terms of their history and cultural legacy.

Most of the African writers are "university wits" and have had the benefit of Western education and training. Many of them are writers as well as critics. With one or two feeble dissenting voices, most of them reject wholesale the theory of "art for art's sake" as a product of the West with little or no relevance to their context. They emphasise the functional and communal value of 'art' as handed down to them by their ancestors. For Achebe, "Art for art's sake is just another piece of deodarised dog-shit . . . art is and was, always in the service of man" [46] and "There is no rigid barrier between the makers and consumers of art (in Africa) . . . Art is a function of society."[47] This integral role of the artist in Africa is juxtaposed with the alienated image of his European counterpart, who according to Achebe "is a pecular specimen in Europe on the fringe of his society and the society in turn suspects his bonafides."[48] Unlike in Africa, the artist in Europe stands outside the mainstream of his society. Ngugi's views on 'art' echo Achebe's when the former says: "African art is oriented to the community" and "Art in African societies was functional."[50]

The views of the two writers are almost identical in relation to the role of the artist and the 'functional' aspect of art. Ngugi and his fellow teachers succeeded in raising a national debate as to the quality, character and nature of literature, art and culture relevant to them. The issues raised are: "what literature, what art, what culture, what values, for whom, for what?" This kind of debate could be relevant in all the third-world countries. Many great people, writers and philosophers have come out with their own theories and solutions to these issues. Karl Marx's observation appears to be relevant to what Ngugi seems to be aiming at: "The philosphers have only interpreted the world in various ways; the point, however, is to change it."[51]

In fact, Ngugi's division of people into two categories as pro-changers and anti-changers, or status-quoists and anti-status-quoists appears to be based on this. Most of Ngugi's writings lend themselves to this kind of interpretation with Ngugi's clear stand in favour of 'pro-changers' as part of his commitment.

Ngugi's most serious commitment lies in his quest for "a socialist order," and "a revolutionary culture" through the processes of the "decolonization of mind" and "decolonization of African Literature." His *Petals of Blood* is an attempt in this direction.

Since modern literature in Africa "has grown against the gory background of European imperialism" scattering Africans in America, West Indies and elsewhere, Ngugi is concerned with his relentless quest for building "a true communal home for all Africans then . . . we have come home."[52] This concern for building a new home on a totally new foundation for all the Africans to live together with a sense of pride, dignity and equality radiates the writings of Ngugi.

Achebe would not go as far as Ngugi in recommending a socialist order as the only panacea for the maladies of Africa. He seems to be of the view that any order, or arrangement (democratic/socialist, or rule by the army) very soon settles down to manifest itself in corrupt and tyrannical forms. Democratic exercise in India and elsewhere in the third-world; the sad spectacle of the fall of the East European countries one after the other and finally the U.S.S.R. itself; and the frequent disintegration of elected and unelected governments in Africa as a result of one coup after another – expose the pitfalls in each system. That is why Achebe would rather recommend the motif of struggle to checkmate power instead of showing his preference for any particular form of governance. This is what he does in his *Anthills of the Savannah*.

V

The novels chosen for discussion in this book are: *Things Fall Apart*, *Arrow of God* and *Anthills of the Savannah* of Achebe and Ngugi's *The River Between*, *A Grain of Wheat*, and *Petals of Blood*. Achebe's *No Longer at Ease* is not part of this study as it is not a political novel in the same way as his other four novels are. *A Man of the People* is also excluded because the problem of political power with which it is concerned finds an indepth and a more profound analysis in its successor, *Anthills of the Savannah*. All the three novels of Achebe are political in tone and substance and are primarily concerned with the problem of power.

The selection of Ngugi's three novels is guided more by the consideration of the nexus rather than the opposition between religion (Christianity) and rebellion as discernible in them. Imposition of Christianity on Africa and its functional role as the "religious ally" of colonialism precipitate the crisis in Ngugi's first published novel, *Weep Not, Child*. The two most recent novels *Devil on the Cross and Matigari*, which were written originally in Gikuyu and translated by Ngugi himself into English later, mark a decisive and final break with Christianity. Hence, these three novels are excluded from the study.

Political power for supremacy and for self-rule dominate the colonial novels of *Things Fall Apart, Arrow of God, The River Between* and to a large extent in *A Grain of Wheat* which culminates in Kenyan Independence. *Petals of Blood* and *Anthills of the Savannah*, the two post-colonial novels, are concerned with the misuse and abuse of power by the native black masters and call for a resolution with a sense of urgency about it through a sustained struggle. The motifs of power and struggle run as an undercurrent in all the novels under discussion and provide a connecting link between Achebe's and Ngugi's fiction. Religion as an additional dimension and as complementary to the motif of struggle or rebellion in Ngugi's fiction is a seminal component of this study. Exploration of Ngugi's and Achebe's fiction on these lines, to my knowledge, has not been attempted so far.

NOTES

1. Hugh Trevor Roper, as quoted by Ali. A. Mazrui, "The Patriot as an Artist," *African Writers on African Writing* (London: Heinemann, 1973), p. 74.
2. C.L. Innes, *The Devil's Own Mirror: The Irishman and the African in Modern Literature* (Washington: Three Continents Press, 1990), p. 4.
3. G.D. Killam, *The Writings of Chinua Achebe* (London: Heinemann Educational Books, 1977), p. 11.
4. *Ibid.*, p. 97.
5. *Ibid.*, p. 98.
6. *Ibid.*, p. 11.
7. C.L. Innes and Bernth Lindfors, ed., *Critical Perspectives on Chinua Achebe* (Washington: Three Continents Press, 1978).
8. *Ibid.*, pp. 6-7.
9. (Cambridge: Cambridge University Press, 1990), p. 2.
10. *Modern Fiction Studies*, Vol. 37, No. 3 (Autumn 1991), p. 459.
11. *Ibid.*, p. 472.
12. (London: KPI, 1980) p. 2.
13. (Bloomington: Indiana University Press, 1972), pp. 18-19.
14. Bernth Lindfors and Bala Kothandaraman, ed., *South Asian Responses to Chinua Achebe* (New Delhi: Prestige, 1993).
15. (London: Heinemann Educational Books, 1980), p. 8.
16. *Ibid.*, p. 7.
17. *Ibid.*, p. 10.
18. *Ibid.*, p. 11.
19. *Ibid.*, p. 72.
20. *Ibid.*, p. 106.
21. (London: The Macmillan Press, 1979), p. 123.
22. *Ibid.*, p. 135.
23. *Ibid.*, p. 124.
24. *Ibid.*, p. 126.
25. *Ibid.*, p. 130.
26. (London: Heinemann Educational Books, 1983), p. 2.
27. *Ibid.*, p. 13.
28. *Loc. cit.*
29. *Loc. cit.*
30. Ngugi wa Thiong'o, "Chinua Achebe: *A Man of the People*," *Homecoming* (London: Heinemann Educational Books, 1972), pp. 53-54.

31. David Cook and Michael Okenimpke, p. 233.
32. *Loc. cit.*
33. *Ibid.*, p. 234.
34. (London: Heinemann, 1985).
35. *Third World Quarterly*, Vol. II, No. I (Jan. 1989), p. 148.
36. *Ibid.*, p.156.
37. Chidi Amuta, *The Theory of African Literature: Implications for Practical Criticism* (London: Zed Books, 1989), p. 100.
38. Achebe's answer to an interviewer, quoted by Kate Turkington in *Studies in English Literature* (London: Edward Arnold, 1977), p. 8.
39. Ngugi wa Thiong'o, "Mau Mau, Violence and Culture," *Homecoming* (London: Heinemann, 1972), p. 28.
40. Chinua Achebe, "The African Writer and the English Language," *Morning Yet on Creation Day* (London: Heinemann, 1972), p. 62.
41. *Ibid.*, p. xiv.
42. Ngugi wa Thiong'o, *Decolonizing the Mind: The Politics of Language in African Literature* (London: Heinemann, 1986), p. 70.
43. *Ibid.*, p. 72.
44. *Ibid.*, p. 71.
45. *Ibid.*, p. 29.
46. Chinua Achebe, *Morning Yet on Creation Day*, p. 19.
47. *Ibid.*, p. 22.
48. *Ibid.*, p. 29.
49. Ngugi, *Homecoming*, p. 7.
50. *Ibid.*, p. 6.
51. Karl Marx, *Theses on Feurbach*.
52. Ngugi, *Homecoming*, p. xix.

Return to the Roots
Things Fall Apart and *The River Between*

> a people's roots were in their traditions going back to the past, the very beginning . . . (*The River Between*, 162)

Both *Things Fall Apart* [1] and *The River Between* [2] seek to discover the cultural ethos of their respective societies. Achebe and Ngugi attempt to explore and identify the roots of their societies and their socio-religious contexts. Both the novels have many common features in terms of their myths, rituals, traditions and the problem of culture conflict.

An attempt is made in this chapter to analyse and examine *Things Fall Apart* and *The River Between* in respect of their interpretation of their cultural identity and ambience. For instance, while *Things Fall Apart* provides a vivid account of the fabric of the Igbos in Eastern Nigeria of 1890s, *The River Between* depicts the texture of life of the Gikuyu people in central Gikuyuland of Kenya in the 1920s.

II

Achebe underlines the indestructible elements of Igbo culture while sensitively depicting its process of disintegration under the impact of the white man's arrival. *Things Fall Apart* is analysed in terms of these enduring values that have the potential of becoming the vital, rejuvenating forces of a resilient and independent Nigerian identity. I will attempt to bring out Achebe's implicit commitment to these values in terms of his views on Igbo myths, beliefs and tradition.

Things Fall Apart seeks to fictionalise the events in Eastern Nigeria of the 1890s. This part of the country is often referred to as Igboland due to the concentration of this particular tribe in the region. The Igbos, by and large, are known for their hard-working and enterprising qualities. One can discern a sort of "cultural uniformity" among the Igbos who "are a single people speaking a number of related dialects with many social features in common." [3] It may not be out of place to provide here a brief account of the political, sociological, religious and cultural aspects of the life of the Igbos for a proper understanding and appreciation of *Things Fall Apart*.

Despite the penetration of Nigeria by the Portuguese in the sixteenth century and transportation of slaves from there in the eighteenth century, the country was free from the infiltration of the European missionaries till the middle of the nineteenth century. Nigeria came under British rule only in the year 1900. Thus, the tenure of both the missionaries and the European colonisers in Nigeria is rather too brief spanning about five decades each.

Unlike in different parts of Nigeria, the institution of Chiefdom is somewhat unfamiliar among the Igbos. The Igbos are a pluralistic society. Decision making power or authority normally rests with the community itself. In other words, a group of elders are involved in matters of crucial decisions at the village community meetings. Besides, the village community is "linked by common shrines and a common myth of descent."[4]

Although each Igbo village is an autonomous political unit, these villages are interlinked and integrated into one another by way of marriages, titled men, Oracles and shrines. Marriages of women within a village community are a taboo. Thus, exogamy serves as an intergrative factor linking several villages creating "a system of affiliations and communications larger than that of the autonomous village."[5]

Men of titles occupy a place of importance in the hierarchy of power in each village. These titles are not conferred by a ruler nor are they awarded by the state. On the other hand, these titles have to be acquired by the individuals concerned either by way of registering success at the village or intra-village level tournaments or by the payment of initiation fee. These men of titles are treated with honour and respect not only by their villages but by the neighbouring villages as well. Yet another significant integrative factor is the presence of oracles and shrines common to many villages.

Igbo religious beliefs and practices also serve as a unifying factor. Three major modes of belief are worth mentioning: worship of the supreme god Chukwu and many other intermediary deities; the worship of ancestors; and finally, the cult of personal god or *Chi*. Chukwu is the supreme god without a shrine or priests. The sky is his abode and he is the god of creation and fertility. He is the final receiver of all the gifts and sacrifices offered to minor deities. Next in the hierarchy is *Ala* or *Ani*, the goddess of earth. She is the owner of all the people, both dead and alive. She is the guardian of the laws of the land and punishes offenders. A constant interaction between the living and the dead is ensured by the presence of *Ala*.

Chi is a sort of personal god or spirit double gifted to an individual at birth by Chukwu. Although the Igbos are a pluralistic society, the individual is provided with enough scope to maipulate his way for the realization of his objectives by means of his *Chi*. According to David Carroll, "the individual is controlled by his *Chi*, but since his role in society has been bargained for he is encouraged to make a success of it." [6] Thus, the Igbo mythology seems to emphasise the principle of dualism as against monism or absolutism. However, what is significant here is that a single autonomous village at its own level as well as a cluster of villages are "held together by a network of relationships, with a common recognition, much stronger than in modern European civilization that the community is greater than the individual and is the source and means of his self-fulfilment." [7]

Things Fall Apart deals vividly with all these aspects of the community life. Thus, Achebe's delineation reminds the world—both African and the European—that Africa had a rich past and legacy:

> African peoples did not hear of culture for the first time from Europeans; that their societies were not mindless but had a philosophy of great depth and value and beauty, that they had poetry and, above all, they had dignity. It is this dignity that many African peoples all but lost in the colonial period, and it is this dignity that they must now regain. [8]

The message of this should be clear for both the natives and the Europeans as well. Thus, Achebe assumes for himself the roles of "a cultural nationalist, explaining the traditions of his people to a largely hostile world, and a teacher, instilling dignity into his own people." [9]

III

Things Fall Apart and *No Longer at Ease* were conceived originally as one novel by Achebe. He felt provoked by the writings of both Conrad and Joyce Cary. *Mister Johnson* of Joyce Cary in particular, appalled him as the novel seeks to portray the African in terms of a savage. Achebe takes on himself the responsibility to rectify the savage image of the African as discernible in European writings. He dismisses *Mister Johnson* as "a most superficial picture . . . not only of the country, but even of the Nigerian character." [10] Hence, as an insider, Achebe attempts to present an authentic interpretation of the African. Instead of writing one comprehensive novel as a rejoinder to *Mister Johnson*, Achebe ended up with two novels by splitting the character of Mister Johnson into two protagonists: viz., Okonkwo of *Things Fall Apart* and his fictional grandson, Obi Okonkwo of *No Longer at Ease*.

Achebe is of the view that the European's understanding of the African, his pysche, sensibility, outlook and attitude is often very limited, lop-sided and shallow and yet he (the European) arrogates to himself the right to understand and interpret the African character.

IV

Things Fall Apart, the title of his first novel, has been carefully chosen by Achebe. The title at once is appealing and striking for several reasons. As pointed out earlier, the novelist wanted to join issue with Joyce Cary's *Mister Johnson* in order to counter the racist account of an outsider dealing with the African situation and the African character.

The title of the novel is abstracted from Yeats's poem, "The Second Coming." Achebe's major concern in *Things Fall Apart*, like that of Yeats in his "Second Coming," is with the decline, disintegration and fall of civilizations. The novelist, obviously, seems to have been influenced by the message in "The Second Coming" and all that the poem seeks to portend in terms of the inherent limitations in each civilization. Yeats is of the view that no civilization can ever beat the laws of time and change despite its frantic effort for perfection and permanence. Ultimately, every civilization collapses paving the way for a new one which will be antithetical to the one it seeks to replace so that a totally new order comes into being. Yeats probably looked at the 1917 October Revolution in Soviet Russia as a formidable force capable of displacing the 2000-year-old Christian civilization in Europe. While both Christianity and Marxism offer hopes of an "ultimate victory" to the adherents of the respective faiths, Yeatsian philosophy emphasises "defeat as inevitable, victory as impermanent and the contending forces as phases of a single, inexhaustible creative energy." [11]

For Umuofia (the fictional locale of *Things Fall Apart*), the Western civilization is no more than a "fabulous formless darkness"[12] and a "mere anarchy let loose on the Umuofian world."[13] Thus, in both the civilizations of Europe and Africa, "the centre cannot hold" and "the falcon cannot hear the falconer." The result: things fall apart.

Things Fall Apart has three parts. The first part comprising 112 pages attempts to celebrate "the ceremony of innocence" symoblized by the Umuofians. This part of the novel is devoted to the depiction of the life of the inhabitants of Umuofia (children of the bush) in terms of their political, cultural, sociological and anthropological aspects. Part-II (35 pages) is a sort of "formless darkness" on account of the intrusion of the

European missionaries in the land of the "innocence." It deals with the depressed life of the protagonist, Okonkwo, as an exile at his mother's place, Mbanta. Part-III (32 pages) assumes the shape of an "anarchy let loose" on the Umuofian world to destroy the native institutions and traditions. This is a stage where the missionaries collaborate with the coloniser or the alien administration. This final section of the novel accounts for the tragic end of the protagonist following his return from exile after a period of seven years.

Although Achebe was provoked to join issue with Conrad's *Heart of Darkness* and Joyce Cary's *Mister Johnson* by way of his maiden novel, *Things Fall Apart*, he also felt the need to recreate the past of Africa in terms of its myths, rituals, customs and traditions. The novelist is, obviously, motivated by the imperative need for the recreation of the African past for the benefit of future generations lest it be thrown into oblivion under the influence of modernity and technological progress. In a way, the novel is a journey into the past and a sort of ritual return to the roots. Commenting on this aspect, Achebe himself observes: "Although I did not set about it consciously in that solemn way I now know that my first book, *Things Fall Apart*, was an act of atonement with my past, the ritual return and homage of a prodigal son."[14]

Things Fall Apart records faithfully the fabric of African life to its minute detail as discernible in the last quarter of the nineteenth century. The novel abounds in details pertaining to the things of the past; for instance, goat-skin bags, drinking-horns, drawing lines in chalk and breaking kola-nuts to greet and honour guests; and finally, spreading broomsticks to settle bride-price and so on and so forth. This part of the past of Africa has already become extinct in face of the growing modernisation everywhere.

In writing *Things Fall Apart*, Achebe is guided by two considerations; to recreate the past of Africa and counter the European version of the African. Unlike the Negritudinists, Achebe does not glorify or romanticize the past of Africa. His account of the continent is both realistic and objective. Jonathan Peters observes: "Achebe succeeds in the delineation of his fictional characters with a touch of objectivity and realism."[15] The novel also presents an authentic picture of the "crumbling past," of its ancestry, its heritage, its warriors and men of titles. It also captures the spirit of the age which is known for its work-ethic and egalitarian values.

Okonkwo proudly exhibits as a trophy "the fifth human head" he acquired in his latest war on behalf of Umuofia. He would drink his palm-wine from this human head on "great occasions such as the funeral of a village celebrity." (10) As part of his preparation for his fatal encounter with the colonial apparatus, Okonkwo closely examines his "war dress," his "smoked rafia skirt, . . . his tall feather head-gear and his shield." (179) A sense of satisfaction flits across his mind as he looks at his war-dress. Goatskin bags, mats, snuff-bottles, drinking horns, lumps of chalk and kola-nuts-all constitute an essential part of each household. For instance, "Okeye unrolled the goatskin which he carried under his arm," (5) and

> Ezinma brought his (Okonkwo's) goatskin bag from the far end of the hut. He searched in it for his snuff-bottle. It was a deep bag and took almost the whole length of his arm. It contained other things apart from his snuff-bottle. There was a drinking horn in it, and also a drinking gourd, and they knocked against each other as he searched . . . then he remembered he had not taken out his snuff-spoon. He searched his bag again and brought out a small, flat ivory spoon, with which he carried the brown snuff to his nostrils.

To greet and honour a guest customarily, Unoka brings "a small wooden disc containing a kolanut, some alligator pepper and a lump of white chalk and drew some lines on the floor, and then painted his big toe." (5) While breaking the kolanut, "Unoka prayed to their ancestors for life and health, and for protection against their enemies." (6) Thus, Achebe tries to capture in the clearest possible terms for the benefit of posterity all that the tradition is said to represent in terms of the antique things, faith and rituals. Chidi Amuta is of the view that *Things Fall Apart* "serves to furnish, albeit fictionally, the essential aspects of pre-literate communalism."[16]

Achebe does not hesitate to point out the flaws which are also part of the African legacy; for instance, abandoning of the twins and the sick in the Evil Forest as they are an abomination to the earth, and the ritual human sacrifices to appease the deities: "Nwoye had heard that twins were put in earthenware pots and thrown away in the forest." (55-56) Unoka

> died of the swelling which was an abomination to the earth goddess. When a man was afflicted with swelling in the stomach and the limbs he was not allowed to die in the house. . . . The sickness was an abomination to the earth, and so the victim could not be buried in her bowels. He died and rotted away above the earth, and was not given the first or the second burial. (16-17)

Ezeudu informs Okonkwo of the decision of Umuofia to sacrifice Ikemefuna as "the Oracle of the Hills and the Caves has pronounced it"

(51) and "the ill-fated lad" is sought to be brutally butchered to appease the Oracle. Thus, Achebe presents, unhesitatingly, the unpleasant side of the community. However, this is a community which "respects age" and "revers achievement." (8) The Umuofians, fight only "just wars" and only with the sanction of the Oracle and never "a war of blame": "it [Umoufia] never went to war unless its case was clear and just and accepted as such by its Oracle . . . it 'would never fight what the Igbo call a fight of blame." (12) Thus, we learn that this is a society in which there is a curious mix of both good and evil; the spiritual and the mundane and finally, the glorious and the gory elements.

Yet another significant facet of the novel is its explication in terms of contrasts and juxtapositions. For instance, Achebe juxtaposes and contrasts both his characters and his major thematic concerns so as to capture the essence of the dichotomy between the past and present; colonial values and civilization vis-a-vis the African mores and moorings. It is worthwhile discussing *Things Fall Apart* on these lines.

The novel seeks to eulogize Okonkwo as a man known for his work-ethic, valour, patriotism and forthrightness. He is juxtaposed and contrasted with his father, Unoka, who is looked down upon as a "loafer," bankrupt and one given to easy ways of living. However, Okonkwo is also irrational and inflexible. Thus, Achebe offers a realistic picture of Okonkwo with all his strength and weaknesses; his nobility and incorrigibility; his sense of patriotism and commitment as well as his obstinacy and orthodoxy. The father-son (Unoka-Okonkwo) juxtaposition is extended to the next generation also so as to cover the lives of Okonkwo and his son Nwoye. The following textual passages illustrate the dichotomy between two generations.

The very opening paragraph of the novel introduces Okonkwo as a man of eminence and popularity and later on the novelist seeks to contrast the unfortunate Unoka, (Okonkwo's father) with Okonkwo. Okonkwo is "well known throughout the nine villages and even beyond. His fame rested on solid personal achievements" and "Okonkwo's fame had grown like a bush-fire in the harmattan . . . He was tall and huge." (3) Unlike his son, Unoka was "lazy and improvident and he was 'a debtor,' and 'owned every neighbour some money, . . . He was tall but very thin and had a slight stoop'." (4) Thus, Okonkwo is introduced to the readers at the very beginning of the novel as a very popular person in the confederation of nine villages called Umuofia and even beyond. Unoka's character is marked by "laziness" and "improvidence." Even in terms of physical features, the son and father are a contrast to each other. While the former is strong and robust, the latter is thin and emaciated.

The contrast does not end here. It is extended further. Okonkwo starts off his life from a scratch to register his fame and success in an aggressive and success-oriented Igbo society. Commenting on the success-obsession of Okonkwo, David Carroll observes: "Driven by this private obsession, Okonkwo has only one aim in life – to succeed, and to succeed in terms of warfare, wrestling, wealth and status."[17]

The greatness of a man in this society is measured in terms of his physical prowess; wealth (barns and grain); number of titles; and finally, number of wives and children. It may be mentioned here that this is a polygamous society. In spite of the fact that he "did not inherit a barn from his father," (7) he manages to become "a wealthy farmer and had two barns full of yams, and had just married his third wife. To crown it all he had taken two titles and had shown incredible prowess in two inter-tribal wars." (7) But, Unoka, "was a failure. He was poor and his wife and children had barely enough to eat. People laughed at him because he was a loafer." (5) The novelist also juxtaposes them in terms of their '*Chi*' governing their lives: "At the most one could say that his *Chi* or personal god was good. But the Igbo people have a proverb that when a man says yes his *Chi* says yes also. Okonkwo said yes very strongly; so his *Chi* agreed." (25) But, Unoka, the "ill fated-man" had a bad *Chi* or personal god, and evil fortune followed him to the grave. (16)

Due to all these reasons, Okonkwo shows "no patience with unsuccessful men. He had no patience with his father." (4) Okonkwo goes up the ladder the hard way and throws himself into work "like one possessed." (17) Fortunately for him, a man in his society is "judged according to his worth and not according to the worth of his father." (7)

The contrast between the son and father is impressively suggested by Chidi Amuta who says:

> the Umuofia society is one in which a very high premium is placed on work – manual work. A man's social estimation is very much determined by the strength of his arm and manifested in his ability to cultivate the land and defeat his opponents in fights and wrestling matches. This accounts for society's adverse estimation of Unoka, . . . In a society where there is no conscious separation between artistic and manual labour, the individual who insists on being identified purely as an artist is doomed to public scorn, open condemnation and alienation.[18]

Not only does Okonkwo have no patience with a father like Unoka, but he even develops a pathological hatred and allergy to all that his father represents in terms of indolence, indebtedness, easy ways of living with no care and concern for fame and success. The very thought or memory of his dead father almost unnerves him. For him, his father is a symbol of "weakness" and failure. He is often "possessed by the fear of his father's contemptible life and shameful death." (17) He is so much obsessed with the failure of his father that this sense of failure injects a fear-psychosis in him. He allows himself to be influenced by this fear-psychosis as an obsession. Unfortunately,

> his whole life was dominated by fear, the fear of failure and of weakness. . . . It was not external but lay deep within himself. It was the fear of himself, lest he should be found to resemble his father, . . . And so Okonkwo was ruled by one passion to hate everything that his father Unoka had loved. One of those things was gentleness and another was idleness. (12-13)

Okonkwo tends to look at things and judge the same from a purely masculine point of view. In other words, he suffers from a "manliness complex." [19] He cannot imagine a man endowed with the finer qualities of "gentleness" and softness. For him, these are nothing but feminine traits. As a matter of fact, his father is a lover of music and he could be passed off for a "superstar . . . in the context of 20th century Western society." [20]

Okonkwo tries to overstretch the thread of "manliness complex" or the masculine-feminine principle to a point of snapping it altogether. Bu Buakei Jabbi's comment in this respect explains how he unwittingly works out his own disintegration. The unbridled "manliness-complex may blaze itself into a veritable *edax rerum*, working out a sinister scheme of suicide and disintegration from within." [21]

Okonkwo tries to judge everybody from this angle of masculinity or manliness. Neither the people of his own Umuofian society nor his mother's kinsmen of Mbanta can pass this standard test of Okonkwo. Hence, they are branded "effeminate," "degenerate" and worthless. Lynn Innes also points out this tragic flaw in Okonkwo when she says: "throughout the novel, Okonkwo judges all action and feeling by that criterion, classifying all that he admires as 'manly,' all that he despises as 'womanly.'" Fear of being called *agbala* like his father is shown to be the motivating force in his life. But it is also clear that Okonkwo is trapped, imprisoned by his classification of everything within such terms. [22]

Okonkwo's twelve-year-old son, Nwoye, is a source of disappointment to him as the boy has soft and gentle qualities in him which he might have inherited from his mother or his grandfather. Okonkwo tries to "correct him by constant nagging and beating" so that the young fellow very soon develops "into a sad-faced youth." (13) According to A.G. Stock,

Okonkwo "is hard to himself and merciless to his family, and has no forbearance for the soft strain in his eldest son, Nwoye."[23] He is often haunted by a feeling whether Nwoye was born to him or if his wife played false to him. He grumbles: "How then could he have begotten a son like Nwoye, degenerate and effemiante? Perhaps he was not his son. No! he could not be. His wife had played him false. . . . But Nwoye resembled his grandfather, Unoka. . . . How could he have begotten a woman for a son?" (140) The thought of his dead father disturbs and unnerves him once again so that he tries to push it "out of his mind." He is no less worried that he resembles his mother. He tells Obierika in a tone of complaint: "there is too much of his mother in him." (60) Obierika responds to this and observes: "Too much of his grand father, Obierika thought, but he did not say it. The same thought also came to Okonkwo's mind." (60)

It is a matter of great shame and concern for Okonkwo that his son does not resemble him in terms of manliness, physical prowess and strength. Hence, he laments that one like him known as the "Roaring Flame" (130) begot a son like "cold impotent ash." (140) The imagery of "Roaring/Flaming Fire" and "cold impotent ash" is an apt description of the qualities in father and the son. Looking at the dying flames of log-fire, he realizes how the roaring flame ultimately becomes cold-ash: "He sighed heavily; and as if in sympathy the smouldering log also sighed. And immediately Okonkwo's eyes were opened and he saw the whole matter clearly. Living fire begets cold, impotent ash. He sighed again, deeply." (140) Bu Buakei Jabbi discusses in detail the imagery of "fire and flames" as attributed to Okonkwo. He says: "Okonkwo's nature and circumstances are most consistently depicted through an imagery of fire."[24] In support of this, he cites a number of relevant passages from the text. For instance, "Okonkwo's fame grows like bush-fire" and "His wives . . . lived in perpetual fear of his fiery temper." (12) Jabbi likens Okonkwo to "a loaded cannon of bottled up emotion, easily ignited into a roaring flame."[25]

Okonkwo tries his best to groom Nwoye by encouraging and telling him "masculine stories of violence and bloodshed" (48) and yet the boy turns out to be a big disappointment for his father. He often wished that his daughter "Ezinma had been a boy," as he feels "she has the right spirit." (60) Okonkwo always has a soft corner for both Ezinma and Ikemefuna. He likes them and is also fond of them. But he always internalizes all such finer feelings of tenderness and love. He would never show such feelings openly. "Perhaps down in his heart Okonkwo was not a cruel man," (12) says the novelist.

Okonkwo's conscious and consistent attempt to erase the image of his dead father from his mind nearly dehumanizes him. He kills Ikemefuna brutally as he "was afraid of being thought weak." (55) The boy used to address him as "father" and Okonkwo was advised against his involvement in the ritual sacrifice of "the ill-fated lad" offered to Umuofia as part of a ransom. One finds it difficult to agree with Stock's version of the Umuofians in the matter of the murder of Ikemefuna by Okonkwo himself. Stock says: "Okonkwo lost no public esteem" [26] due to his killing of Ikemefuna. But the fact is that Umuofia does not approve of the murder of a boy by one treated as "father." Ezeudu, who informs Okonkwo of the decision of Umuofia to kill Ikemefuna, also cautions him: "They will take him outside Umuofia as is the custom, and kill him there. But I want you to have nothing to do with it. He calls you his father." (51) This caution is given before the murder of the boy. Later, following the murder of the boy by Okonkwo, Obierika expresses his sense of anguish on behalf of the community for this dastardly act. Obierika's comment is worth recording here: "And let me tell you one thing, my friend. If I were you I would have stayed at home. What you have done will not please the Earth. It is the kind of action for which the goddess wipes out whole families." (60-61)

The enormity and magnitude of the crime committed by Okonkwo is such that the punishment is not confined to the individual offender alone but even the community also bears the brunt of it. The net result of the crime is that it sets in the process of alienation of Nwoye from his father. It is true that "*Things Fall Apart* is largely concerned with a father/son conflict, a conflict which is linked to that between warrior and poet, pragmatism and feeling as well as between two kinds of language, the dogmatic and the poetic." [27] Okonkwo's hatred for his dead father is in the nature of a dichotomy between "warrior" and an artist (Unoka was fond of and dedicated to music). Nwoye's alienation from his father is due to a seminal maladjustment between an "inflexible" father and a tender-hearted son invested with the sensibility of a sensitive poet. The "rollicking music" of the missionaries' songs touches and moves the very core of the young boy's being: "gay and rollicking tunes of evangelism . . . had the power of plucking at silent and thirsty chords in the heart of an Igbo man." (133)

> It was the poetry of the new religion, something felt in the marrow. The hymn about brothers who sat in darkness and in fear seemed to answer a vague and persistent question that haunted his young soul—the question of the twins crying in the bush and the question of Ikemefuna who was killed. He [Nwoye] felt a relief within as the hymn poured into his parched soul. The words of the hymn were

> like the drops of frozen rain melting on the dry palate of the panting earth. Nwoye's callow mind was greatly puzzled. (134)

The hymns of the missionaries seem to provide answers to the problems that Nwoye's "puzzled mind" has been looking for. True, they are like "the drops of frozen rain" on the dry "palate and the parched soul" of Nwoye also. Hence, "Nwoye . . . rejects the Igbo set of beliefs to become a Christian."[28]

Okonkwo, unfortunately, never realizes the greatness of the Igbo tradition which is quite resilient and flexible in terms of the role of the individual vis-a-vis the importance of the community. While an individual enjoys the freedom to pursue his objectives, the community seeks to regulate and guide his behaviour. Thus, both the individual and the community are interlinked and subservient to each other. David Carroll's comment in this regard is worth mentioning here. According to Carroll, "This flexibility is seen . . . in the absence of a central authority, the rejection of absolute laws, and the fluidity of village groupings."[29] The individual in the Igbo context has his relevance and importance only in relation to his community and not as one apart from it. Okonkwo's tendency to place himself above the community leads to his alienation from it. Unoka's warning to him during a very bad season of floods and drought turns out to be propehetic. Unoka said to him: "you have a manly and a proud heart. A proud heart can survive a general failure because such a failure does not prick its pride. It is more difficult and more bitter when a man fails alone." (23)

The tragedy of Okonkwo is that he does not hesitate to do a thing all alone. He chooses to fight 'alone' and on behalf of the community against the colonial administration. He is also aware that his community is not prepared to support him in his fight. In a fit of near madness, he beheads the messenger of the white man with his matchet to the dismay and shock of the entire community. He realizes the possible consequences of his action in killing the messenger and decides on the course of suicide rather than allow himself to be hanged by the white administration, which often "judged cases in ignorance." (158) Thus, Okonkwo awaits the similar fate of his father for whom no funeral could be arranged. Okonkwo embodies the Igbo-traits of sturdiness, strength and self-dignity. The negative aspect, however, was his fear of 'failure.' The 'manliness-complex' appears to dry up the milk of human-kindness in him as evidenced in his merciless killing of Ikemefuna against the advice of Ezeudu, a village elder. His irrational and almost pathological allergy to affection which he considers to be a form of weakness nearly dehumanizes him. He had a fiery disposition; was an iron man, but he failed to take the community with him. He lacked the leadership quality to rally and consolidate the native forces against the aggression of the white man. His rash and impulsive act of killing the whiteman's messenger, however heroic in itself, amounted to an admission of collective defeat – a signal of community's surrender and colonial triumph.

Achebe also juxtaposes two of his missionaries, Mr. Brown and Mr. Smith so as to bring out the striking dissimilarities between them. While the former is very accommodating and open-minded in his interaction with the religious pursuits and beliefs of the natives, the latter is very impatient and irrational in respect of the natives and their traditions. In fact, Mr. Brown used to restrain his flock very firmly "from provoking the wrath of the clan." (161) Consequently, "Mr. Brown's school produced quick results" and his "mission grew from strength to strength." (164)

Mr. Smith, Brown's successor, is a different specimen altogether. He not only "condemned openly Mr. Brown's policy of compromise and accommodation. He saw things as black and white. And black was evil. He saw the world as a battlefield in which the children of light were locked in mortal conflicts with the sons of darkness." (166) Thus, Mr. Smith shares with Okonkwo the qualities of impatience and inflexibility. While Okonkwo is obstinate, Mr. Smith is arrogant. According to David Carroll, he "is a literalist, as adamant an authoritarian in his beliefs as Okonkwo." [30] Moreover, his world "is a Manichean one" sharply distinguished in terms of good and evil, similar to the world described by Fanon. [31] Both Okonkwo and Mr. Smith precipitate the crisis and ignite fire in their own characteristic manner. Apart from the juxtaposition of two white missionaries, Achebe also seeks to contrast both the native African concept of religion and the Christian faith.

Mr. Brown used to enter into discourse with the natives to learn about their religious beliefs. Akunna, a village elder, counters effectively the argument of Mr. Brown in respect of 'fear' which forms part of both the religions. The dialogue between them is as follows:

> Mr. Brown: You are afraid of Chukwu. In my religion Chukwu is a loving father and need not be feared by those who do His will.
>
> Akunna: But we must fear Him when we are not doing His will. And who is to tell His will? It is too great to be known. (163)

'Fear,' thus, is a vital element in both the religions despite emphatic denial of the same by the Christian religious priests. "Fear of the Lord is the beginning of wisdom" is a dictum which reinforces the argument of

Akunna while rendering the point of view of Mr. Brown ineffectual.

The anonymous D.C. (District Commissioner) is yet another interesting character whose knowledge of the native customs and beliefs is exposed as shallow and absurd despite his tall claims as a "student of primitive customs." (186) He planned to do a book dealing with the natives and the caption he chooses for his proposed book is: "The Pacification of the Primitive Tribes of The Lower Niger." The story of Okonkwo, he feels, could constitute a whole chapter in his book. But, later on, he changes his mind so as to devote no more than "a paragraph" to him. This only testifies to the white man's innate prejudice in the assessment of the dead hero. The D.C. has his heirs in Mr. Green of *No Longer at Ease* and Captain Winterbottom of *Arrow of God*. *Things Fall Apart* is a great classic, and an epic in honour of a great patriot, a man of integrity and commitment albeit his flaws. One cannot miss what Obeirika says in an emotional outburst while referring to the tragic death of Okonkwo at the end of the novel: "That man was one of the greatest men in Umuofia. You drove him to kill himself; and now he will be buried like a dog." (187)

V

The River Between sheds light on the importance of love, education and the need for reconciliation between antagonistic beliefs represented by Christianity on the one hand and indigenous tribal beliefs and values on the other. The original title of the novel was to be "The Black Messaiah," but later on Ngugi changed it to *The River Between.* The river Honia divides the Christianized half of the tribe from the traditional Gikuyu tribe. But it also symbolizes sustenance and new growth.

The River Between is sought to be analysed in terms of the ancient wisdom embedded in the "ways of the hills" and the creation myth of the Gikuyu people and a strong yearning for peace and reconciliation between the two hostile groups inhabiting the two ridges of Kameno and Makuyu.

The seminal issue in *The River Between* is the significance of land which is not only the source of livelihood, but it also serves as the medium of forging spiritual bonds with the people. The novel revolves round the Gikuyu creation myth according to which Murungu, the Gikuyu God, told the people: "This land I give to you, O man and woman. It is yours to rule and till." (2) It is widely believed that Gikuyu and Mumbi, the original parents of the clan, moved around the places of Kameno. A small hill surrounded by bushes on the banks of the Honia is often shown as evidence of the presence of Gikuyu and Mumbi at this "sacred grove" in the bygone days. The place is considered holy and held in great awe and reverence by the Gikuyu people. Answering a query in an interview, Ngugi remarked: "it is more than the material; it is not just because of economic possibilities, it is almost akin to spiritual."[32]

While the land was offered as a gift to the people by Murungu, Mugo wa Kabiro, an ancient seer of the land, warned them about the infiltration and desecration of the land by strangers. He said: "There shall come a people with clothes like butterflies." (2) But the people did not heed his prophecy. On the other hand, he was called an "imposter." Disgusted, he left the place only to be "heard of in the land beyond" later. (2)

Mugo, the seer, Wachoiri, the warrior, aand Kamiri, the man of magic, were all sent to Kameno by Murungu. Kameno is proud of these legendary figures. However, these great sons of the soil were considered strangers in their time in their own land. It is also believed that Chege, the father of Waiyaki, is a descendant of Mugo. Elders feared and respected him and "he was at the head of every important ceremony." (8) While some believed that he "had the gift of magic, some others felt that 'he was a seer and Murungu often spoke to him'." (8)

Chege takes Waiyaki to the hills of the land, to the "sacred grove"; explains to him "the hidden things of the hills" (18); and the matriarchal origins of the clan; and also shows him the "snow-capped" Kerinyaga (Mount Kenya), the seat of Murungu. Chege reveals many more important things to Waiyaki. He says: "We are his [Mugo's] offspring. His blood flows in your veins." (22) But, the seer was rejected by the people of the ridges. He says further:

> Now listen my son . . . for this is the ancient prophecy . . . when the white man came and fixed himself in Siriana, I warned all the people. But they laughed at me. May be I was hasty. . . . Salvation shall come from the hills. From the blood that flows in me. I say from the same tree, a son shall rise. And his duty shall be to lead and save the people! (24)

Chege also warns his son saying, "You are the last in the line." (23) Chege wants his son to go to the Siriana Mission school to learn the wisdom and secrets of the white man. He says: "Arise. Heed the prophecy. Go to the Mission place. Learn all the wisdom and all the secrets of the white man. But do not follow his vices. Be true to your people and the ancient rites." (24) The advice is strikingly similar to what Ezeulu imparted to his son about the superiority of the white man in education, technology and statecraft. If the natives choose to survive with dignity and independence in the comity of nations, they need to learn the modern skills and beat the white man in his own game.

This is precisely what the Indian leaders like Ram Mohan Roy and others emphasised to free the natives from ignorance and superstition. Tilak, Gandhi and Nehru were very much the products of Western education. They became the architects of a resurgent nation and liberated India.

But, the adolescent Waiyaki has his own apprehensions about the larger than life role his father has carved out for him and observes: "But – but – they do not know me. I am a child and they rejected Mugo. . ." (24) True, Mugo was not only rejected but branded an "imposter." Chege, in his time, was only "laughed at" when he tried to warn his people when the missionaries infiltrated into the neighbouring Siriana, Makuyu and other places. Waiyaki is always conscious and haunted by the fact that he also awaits the similar fate of Mugo and his father. Herein lies the tragedy of Waiyaki as he goes much farther in his designs than his predecessors because of his peculiar situation and context.

The deep-seated rivalry between the ridges of Kameno and Makuyu on the issue of leadership of the clan gets accentuated by the presence of the missionaries in Makuyu. While Kameno is known for its legendary heroes and the traditional wisdom of the hills, Makuyu has already come under the influence of the missionaries. The very opening page of the novel seeks to capture the rivalry between the ridges. Robson observes: "In *The River Between,* Ngugi succeeds in evoking the atmosphere of the ridges and chronicling the traditions and customs they embrace."[31] The ridges "Faced each other, like two rivals ready to come to blows in a life and death struggle for the leadership of this isolated region." (1)

VI

The antagonism between the ridges takes a serious turn on the issue of circumcision. Circumcision of both the sexes has several facets to it. It is a sort of initiation into womanhood and manhood respectively. It is an emotional issue for the Gikuyus. The dripping of blood at the time of circumcision on the banks of the Honia links them to the land emotionally and spiritually. "Circumcision of women," in particular, "was not important as a physical operation. It was what it did inside a person." (163) Besides, it is "the central rite in the Gikuyu way of life." (44)

Muthoni, the daughter of Joshua, the militant catechist, rebels against her father so as to win for herself the freedom of getting circumcised at Kameno, her aunt's place. Muthoni is guided by more than one consideration in opting for circumcision. She would like to enjoy the best of both the worlds of Christian faith and also the pagan rites. Thus, she hopes to integrate the two contradictory faiths. She gives her reasons why she feels the need for circumcision. She shares the same with her sister, Nyambura:

> Father and mother are circumcised. Are they not Christians? . . . I too have embraced the white man's faith. . . . I know it is beautiful, oh! so beautiful to be initiated into womanhood. You learn the ways of the tribe. Yes, the white man's God does not quite satisfy me. I want, I need somethig more. My life and your life are here, in the hills, . . . (29-30)

This is how she defends the act of circumcision. But, unfortunately, the wound of Muthoni caused by circumcision becomes too serious to heal. Waiyaki takes her to the Mission hospital at Siriana. But it is already too late. She tells her sister while the latter visits her at the hospital: "You too will have to make a choice one day." (58) This statement by Muthoni is very crucial not only from her view alone, but it also provides an insight into the very philosophy of Ngugi about the "choice" one has to exercise in one's life in relation to one's community or society. The need to make one's choice in the course of one's life is given a more profound treatment in his *Petals of Blood*.

Muthoni experiences a sense of contentment that she has been able to marry her Christian faith to her pagan rites. She says: "I am still Christian . . . a Christian in the tribe. I am a woman and will grow big and healthy in the tribe." (61) As she breathes her last, she turns to Waiyaki and says: "Tell Nyambura I see Jesus. And I am a woman beautiful in the tribe." But the people, unable to understand why she has taken recourse to circumcision, kept asking themselves: "Why did she do it? Why? And even for Waiyaki the question remained 'Why?'" (61) Several people attributed various reasons for Muthoni's death. Her father placed a curse on her for her disobedience and the way "she had sold herself to the devil." (62) For the Christians, "the death of Muthoni forever confirmed the barbarity of Gikuyu customs." (63) They also felt that she "was an evil spirit sent to try the faithful." (67-68) The Gikuyu people believed that Muthoni "had not actually died of the wound, but that she had been poisoned by the missionaries." (67) Her death was ominous for them and hence, any form of association with the new faith is nothing but evil. "This new faith," they thought "had contaminated the hills and Murungu was angry." (67) Moreover, it "was a punishment to Joshua. It was also a punishment to the hills. It was a warning to all, to stick to the ways of the ridges, to the ancient wisdom of the land, to its ritual and song." (62) Chege is worried that his son got involved in it. In any case, it "did not augur well for the future," (63) and nobody knew for certain what the death portended.

The name of Muthoni becomes a legend very soon. Like Santiago of Hemingway's *Old Man and the Sea*, Muthoni is "dead but not destroyed." [34] Ngugi himself interprets her death in terms of "martyrdom." [35] Robson adds further: "her death sparks off in the ridges the sort of conflict going on in the mind of Waiyaki." [36] Commenting on the death of Muthoni, Lloyd Williams observes: "Christianity cannot be meaningful to her if it attempts to meet her outside the tribe, outside of her life in the tribe." [37] In other words, "What Muthoni wants is both Christianity and the tribe." [38]

Muthoni wanted to integrate the conflicting faiths of Christianity and the ways of the tribe. But in the process, she pays a heavey price – of her life itself. Her death also further aggravates the tension between the ridges. And "The War was now on." (65)

VII

The rivalry between Kabonyi, an elder of Makuyu and Waiyaki is comparable to the rivalry between Nwaka and Ezeulu in *Arrow of God* for the leadership of the clan. Apart from Chege and Waiyaki, Kabonyi is also aware of the ancient prophecy about the saviour of the tribe hailing from the hills. Chege is a visionary and Waiyaki is too sentimental and idealistic. But Kabonyi is very shrewd and pragmatic. The death of Muthoni, followed closely by the death of Chege, prompts him to change his *modus operandi* to grab the leadership of the ridges from Waiyaki. Kabonyi, who has been a convert to Christianity for long, abandons his Christian faith and embraces once again "the ways of the hills" with a renewed vigour. He also forms the Kiama, an oath meant to preserve the purity of tribal customs. He very subtly involves Waiyaki in the Kiama with a view to undoing him at an appropriate time.

Waiyaki very soon acquires an excellent image as Teacher. Apart from spreading education, he is also guided by the need for "reconciliation between Joshua's followers and the others" as the "gulf between them was widening and Waiyaki wanted to be the instrument of their coming together." (104) He successfully conveys this message at the well organised Parents' Committee Meeting. The people are convinced of Waiyaki's sincerity and begin to imagine a "Saviour" in him. They know that he had "opened the eyes of the people. He had awakened the sleeping lions. They would now roar, roar to victory. The children were getting learning." While Waiyaki tries to impress the parents on the need for more schools, buildings and teachers, Kabonyi draws their attention to the more pressing need of the hour – to drive away the white man from their land. He questions the wisdom in white man's education. He appeals to their "pride and manhood." He exhorts them not to be misled by a youth. Although Kabonyi succeeds partially in convincing the people about his plans, it is Waiyaki who has a sway over the people at this stage.

Meanwhile, Waiyaki gets involved in love with Nyambura, another daughter of Joshua. Despite his success in organising many schools and his image as a Teacher, Waiyaki also is driven by a passion for love through which he hopes to find his identity and fulfilment. Nyambura and he would meet clandestinely on the banks of the Honia, the spot of circumcision. Once he takes her in his arms and embraces her. She does not resist. On the other hand, she tries to merge her being in him for a while as though to alleviate her loneliness and to free herself from the burden and weight of her father. He proposes himself to her and wants to know whether she will marry him. She is puzzled. Unlike her sister Muthoni, she does not want to rebel. In spite of herself, she says 'no' to him and regrets later for having rejected him. She, however, has no qualms in accepting him finally.

Waiyaki's movements are closely spied on by Kamau, Kabonyi's son. While Kabonyi is a rival to Waiyaki in the matter of leadership of the ridges, Kamau finds a rival in Waiyaki in his love for Nyambura. Waiyaki's mother, in particular, is greatly disturbed at his involvement in love with an uncircumcised girl of a different faith. She also warns him about the power of the Kiama and the wrath of the people. She says: "Fear the voice of the Kiama. It is the voice of the people. When the breath of the people turns against you, it is the greatest curse you can ever get." (141) The talk about marrying Nyambura by his well-wishers pricks him all the more in the light of her rejection of him. Meanwhile, Miriamu, Nyambura's mother, tells her how she feels about her involvement with Waiyaki. She says: "We do not want any more trouble in this house. I cannot bear it not after Muthoni." (131) Her father warns her more severely in his characteristic manner: "If I hear that you have been seen with that young devil again you no longer live in this house." (132) The harsh treatment of her father is like a pain in a wound. She regrets her obedience to her father and her loyalty to her faith. She feels that "because of her obedience she had lost the one man whom she loved. And with him her salvation." (133)

While Waiyaki and Nyambura are involved passionately in love with each other, despite opposition from their parents and the community at large for obvious reasons, the situation in the ridges begins to take a turn for the worse. On the one hand, the Kiama, under the influence of

Kabonyi, is all set to take on the alien administration and to fight for the restoration of the lost lands. On the other, Waiyaki is still obsessed with the need for "reconciliation, tolerance and unity." (125) He does not like to be identified with either side. Meanwhile, a hut belonging to a Joshua's follower is burnt precipitating the crisis.

Waiyaki learns that the followers of Kabonyi are out to create problems at Joshua's place. Waiyaki rushes there foolishly to warn the latter about the impending danger to his family. Nyambura could not stand Waiyaki being humiliated and turned out of her house by her father. At last, she picks up enough courage to leave her father's house for good so as to live with "her black Messiah, sent from heaven after Muthoni's death to . . . rescue her from disintegration." (154) Finally, her love for Waiyaki triumphs over her obedience to her father. She accepts the hand of Waiyaki and walks out surprising the latter and shocking her father. He places a curse on her: "You will come to an untimely end." (157)

At this stage, Waiyaki realizes that he is required by the circumstances to exercise "his choice between the girl and the tribe" (159) although he would be happier to have both. While he is agitated about this crucial choice, Nyambura "felt at peace" at his place. She feels more secure and sure of herself here, ironically though. As far as she is concerned, her quest is over. Waiyaki also feels that his quest for identity and fulfilment is over the moment he finds himself accepted in the warm embrace of Nyambura, despite her hesitation in giving her consent to marry him. "Love" is the medium through which they seek each other's fulfilment.

Waiyaki, like his creator Ngugi, seems to endorse the view that a religious faith of people has to grow organically from within. The message of *The River Between* is: "a people's religion and a people's way of life must be one; each must grow out of the other. Either one by itself is incomplete." [39] Both Nyambura and Muthoni realize ultimately that the kind of Christian faith they are subjected to, cannot sustain them. While Muthoni attempts to integrate her Christian faith to her pagan rite of circumcision, Nyambura abandons her Christian faith totally so as to find her "peace."

Miriamu, Joshua's wife, learnt as a necessity and out of a compulsion the value of Christian "submission" unquestioningly. For her, Christianity is "a religion learnt and accepted; inside [her] the true Gikuyu woman was sleeping." (39) Substantiating this idea, Lloyd Williams expounds the orthodox view. "The religious law demands that man accept ideas and dogmas; that he believe in doctrines and traditions, the acceptance of which is salvation."[40]

Joshua, the militant catechist, also clutches to his faith blindly and dogmatically. He cannot understand how anybody can have his "feet on two roads at the same time." (99) There seems to be a sad logic in this statement of Joshua. In this light, the fate of those wanting to integrate and reconcile the divergent faiths in the best interests of a community cannot be anything other than tragic. This holds good in the case of Muthoni, Nyambura and Waiyaki. It is an irony that Joshua's house, which he considers to be a stable centre with a "strong Christian foundation" (34) is disrupted from within because of his militancy and irrationality in the pursuit of his religious beliefs. His house is disrupted and broken as he tries to impose "an uncompromising religious law" from above. According to Waiyaki, Joshua "had clothed himself with a religion decorated and smeared with everything *white.* He renounced his past and cut himself away from those life giving traditions of the tribe." (163)

VIII

Waiyaki is summoned to the Kiama to clarify his position in relation to Nyambura. Earlier, he is stripped of his position from the school administration. He realizes rather late that "the new awareness [among people] wanted expression at a political level" and that "education for an oppressed people is not all." (162) By now people are concerned more with serious issues like the alienation of land from them and payment of taxes to a government about which they know nothing. Kabonyi fully exploits these things to his advantage and succeeds in turning the elders against Waiyaki.

Nyambura, who was kidnapped from the house of Waiyaki by the men of Kabonyi, is produced before the Kiama. Despite his awareness that his position has become vulnerable, Waiyaki tries his best to defend himself before the Kiama. He takes pains to trace the history of the tribe and its geneology. He implores them to stand united at this hour of crisis. He says: "We are all children of Mumbi and we must fight together in one political movement, or else we perish and the white man will always be on our back. Can a house divided against itself stand?" (171) The Kiama would no longer care for what Waiyaki has to say. He is asked to deny Nyambura who, for him, "looked like a lamb on the altar of sacrifice." (173) Waiyaki cannot bring himself to deny her. The result: both Waiyaki and Nyambura are handed over to the Kiama for the final trial and possibly execution since it felt that Waiyaki defiled the ways of the hills by his association with an uncircumcised girl of an alien faith. People leave the place with a sense of guilt.

IX

There are many things in common between *Things Fall Apart* and *The River Between*. Both the novels seek to go back to the roots of their respective societies so as to delineate their past in terms of its myths, traditions and rituals. Both the protagonists – Okonkwo and Waiyaki – are cast in a tragic mould. Both the novels are concerned with the presence of the early missionaries and the resultant culture conflict. The element of curse – a father's curse is common in both the novels. While Okonkwo places a curse on his first son, Nwoye, for the latter's conversion to Christianity, Joshua places curse on his only two daughters since they chose to rebel against the Christian faith. As per the latter's curse, both the daughters "meet an untimely end." While the Egwugwu destroy the house of the white man's God in *Things Fall Apart*, the followers of Kabonyi set on fire the house belonging to a Joshua's follower. Both Okonkwo and Waiyaki suffer from a sort of fear-psychosis.

Apart from some of these things, one can find situations which are almost similar in *Things Fall Apart* and *The River Between*. Both the novelists depict the arrival of the missionaries and the generous attitude of the natives to them in the same vein: In *Things Fall Apart*, we are told "He (representing the missionaries) came quietly and peaceably with his religion. We were amused at his foolishness and allowed him to stay. He has put a knife on the things that held us together and we have fallen apart." (160) The passage offers an interesting comparison with its counterpart in *The River Between* with reference to the arrival of missionaries in Siriana where "the men of God came peacefully. They were given a place . . . they have invited their brothers to come and take all the land. Our country is invaded. This government post behind Makuyu is a plague in our midst. And this hut-tax." (174) In *Things Fall Apart*, the thrust of the white man is to cause dissensions among the natives through his religion. In *The River Between*, the white man's efforts are directed at alienating the people from their lands.

Both the novelists have protagonists whose popularity is always on the rise till they fall. For instance, "Okonkwo's fame had grown like a bushfire in the harmattan (in all the nine villages and beyond)." (1) Whereas Waiyaki's "fame grew from ridge to ridge and spread like fire in dry bush." (105)

The most striking similar incident in both the novels is a decisive action by the protagonist Okonkwo in *Things Fall Apart* in killing the white man's messenger and the deliberate and bold bid by Muthoni in *The River Between* opting for circumcision. In the former, the protagonist realizes that he has no alternative other than suicide in the face of a certain execution by the white man. His death by hanging implies the disintegration of his society. Muthoni's circumcision not only results in her death but precipitates the matters between the antagonistic ridges. In both cases, the people of their respective communities are puzzled and they end up asking themselves as to what prompted them to act the way they did. Following the execution of the white man's messenger, Okonkwo heard voices asking: "Why did he do it?"

In a similar situation, following the death of Muthoni who succumbs to her wound of circumcision, people kept asking themselves: "Why did she do it? Why? And even for Waiyaki the question remained 'Why'?" (161) Perhaps the answer to this 'Why' is embedded in the noble impulsion and intention of the two protagonists. Okonkwo rebelled against the arrogance of power and of bossism shown by the foreign intruders who indulged in blatant interference in their domestic affairs. His killing of the white man's messenger symbolizes the revolutionary ardour of the patriotic native forces to overthrow and annihilate the white hegemony. Muthoni's circumcision is a valiant gesture of a person who would willingly undergo martyrdom for reconciling the hostile factions. The supreme irony of this sacrifice, however, in both the cases is the alienation and disaffection it produced among their own people. The dead heroes are left unhonoured and unsung. Some of these passages suggest that Ngugi was overwhelmingly influenced by *Things Fall Apart* and he also acknowledges the same.

X

It is interesting and in place to note the contrasting personalities of Okonkwo and Waiyaki. While Okonkwo is a staunch believer in tribal customs, Waiyaki is conscious of the pitfalls of blind and orthodox beliefs in all that is old and has a compulsive urge for education and enlightenment to counter the regressive features of tribal fetish and superstition. Okonkwo is dead set against all that is new and that which emanates from the white man and heaps a curse on his son who is attracted to missionary culture and education.

If anything, Okonkwo resembles Kabonyi, a fanatical convert from the Christian to the tribal belief -- who holds everything that is tribal to be sacrosanct and detests everything that smacks of colonial culture. Okonkwo indulges in a violent killing of the white man's messenger and utters imprecations on the white man's institutions of religion and education. He, however, does not have the organising ability of Kabonyi to rally the native forces under the banner of anti-colonial and anti-imperialist struggle. Waiyaki, in a small measure, to strike an analogy, is Gandhian in approach and ultimately falls a martyr to his own convictions. He is a messianic, idealist figure who lacks in political acumen and has no plan of political action to range the nationalistic forces against the white hegemony and lead a mass movement like what Gandhi did in launching his Civil Disobedience campaign.

Okonkwo is all brawn lacking in thinking faculty to reason out things and evolve a strategy for the community against the white intruder. The heroic streak in him, however, is a life of action, industry, adventure and achievement. He suppresses emotion, sentiment and even affection regarding these as unmanly and effeminate.

While Ngugi resents the white invasion that dispossesses the natives of their lands by white settlers and disinherits them from their cultural roots, Achebe underscores in his subtle artistic way the positive features of native culture to show that "Africa was not a primordial void but has a history, a religion and a civilization."

NOTES

1. Chinua Achebe, *Things Fall Apart* (London: William Heinemann, 1958; New Delhi: Allied, 1988).
2. Ngugi wa Thiong'o, *The River Between* (London: Heinemann Educational Books, 1965).
3. David Carroll, *Chinua Achebe* (London: The Macmillan Press, 1980), p. 14.
4. *Ibid.,* p. 15.
5. *Ibid.*, p. 16.
6. *Ibid.*, p. 18.
7. A.G. Stock, "Yeats and Achebe," *Critical Perspectives on Chinua Achebe,* ed. C.L. Innes and Bernth Lindfors, pp. 87-88.
8. Chinua Achebe, "The Role of the Writer in a New Nation," *Nigeria Magazine* (1964), p. 1577. Koloawole Ogungbesan, "Politics and the African Writer," *Critical Perspectives on Chinua Achebe*, p. 38.
9. Koloawole Ogunbesan, p. 38.
10. As quoted by C.L. Innes in *The Devil's Own Mirror*, p. 57.
11. A.G. Stock, p. 86.
12. *Ibid*., p. 87.
13. *Ibid*., p. 91.
14. Chinua Achebe, "Named for Victoria, Queen of England," *Morning Yet on Creation Day,* p. 70.

15. Jonathan A. Peters, *A Dance of Masks: Senghar, Achebe, Soyinka* (Washington: Three Continents Press, 1978).
16. Chidi Amuta, "History and the Dialects of Narrative in the African Novel," *The Theory of African Literature* (London: Zed Books, 1989), p. 130.
17. David Carroll, pp. 39-40.
18. Chidi Amuta, pp. 130-51.
19. Bu Buakei Jabbi, "Fire and Transition in *Things Fall Apart*," *Critical Perspectives on Chinua Achebe*, p. 135.
20. Chidi Amuta, p. 131.
21. *Ibid.*, p. 136.
22. Innes, *The Devil's Own Mirror*, p. 76.
23. A.G. Stock, p. 88.
24. Bu Buakei Jabbi, p. 136.
25. *Ibid.*, p. 137.
26. A.G. Stock, p. 88.
27. Innes, *The Devil's Own Mirror*, p. 71.
28. *Loc. cit.*
29. David Carroll, p. 38.
30. *Ibid.*, p. 55
31. Innes, *The Devil's Own Mirror*, p. 83.
32. Ngugi wa Thiong'o, interviewed by Dennis Duerden in *African Writers Talking* (London: Heinemann, 1972), p. 123
33. C.B. Robson, *Ngugi wa Thiong'o*, p. 1.
34. Robert Sermuga, "A Mirror of Integration," *Protest and Conflict in African Literature* (London: Heinemann, 1969), p. 75.
35. *Ibid.*, p. 11.
36. *Ibid.*, p. 9.
37. Lloyd E. Williams, "Religion and Life in Ngugi's *The River Between,*" *African Literature Today,* Vol. V (1971), p. 55.
38. *Ibid.*, p. 56.
39. *Ibid.*, p. 64.
40. *Ibid.*, p. 62.

Predicament of the Priest: *Arrow of God*

> Tell the white man that Ezeulu will not be anybody's chief, except Ulu. [1]

Like *Things Fall Apart*, *Arrow of God* is also concerned with the socio-cultural milieu of the people prior to British occupation. The novel seeks to explicate in much greater depth the myths, traditions of Umuaro (the fictional locale of the novel) and the problem of culture-conflict than *Things Fall Apart* does. While *Things Fall Apart* mirrors the Igbo society of the last quarter of the 19th century, *Arrow of God* deals with the colonial situation of the same community in the first quarter of the present century.

Both Okonkwo and Ezeulu, the protagonists of *Things Fall Apart* and *Arrow of God*, have many things in common in terms of their commitment to their respective communities, sincerity of purpose, a measure of defiance and obstinacy against the forces which seek to challenge their presence and power. Both are guided by 'fear' and are 'loners' in their own way despite being leaders of their clans. While Okonkwo is essentially "a man of action," Ezeulu is a man of thought. The former does not read the writing on the wall whereas the latter is perceptive and alive to the realities in the context of the white man and his government. The former is adamant, blunt and bellicose in all that he says and does. One can easily guess the line of action he is likely to take in a given situation. Ezeulu is subtle, unpredictable and mysterious and plays his cards close to his chest all the time.

Arrow of God fictionalises an actual incident documented in *The History of Umuchu* [2] by Simon Nnolim. According to an account in this book, Ezeagu, a priest declined the offer of chieftaincy by the colonial administration. He was imprisoned for his defiance and he refused to eat the sacred Yams which he was to consume as part of his ritual meal. While Okonkwo perishes in his attempt to emerge as the leader of his clan by running his head against the giant colonial apparatus, Ezeulu's predicament lies in his ambition to retain his position as the unrivalled leader of his community in both religious and political matters of Umuaro.

The novel revolves round Ezeulu, the custodian deity of Umuaro. Ulu was created and installed as the principal deity of Umuaro out of a dire security need. Its history is as follows:

> the six villages – Umuachala, Umunneora, Umuagu, Umuezeani, Umuogwugwu and Umuisiuzo – lived as different peoples, and each worshipped its own deity. Then the hired soldiers of Abam used to strike in the dead of night, set fire to the houses and carry men, women and children into slavery. Things were so bad for the six villages that their leaders came together to save themselves. They hired a strong team of medicine-men to install a common deity for them. This deity which the fathers of the six villages made was called Ulu. Half of the medicine was buried at a place which became Nkwo market and the other half thrown into the stream which became Mili Ulu. The six villages then took the name of Umuaro, and the priest of Ulu became their Chief Priest. From that day they were never again beaten by an enemy. (14-15)

The functions of Ezeulu as the chief priest are, in the main, religious – to perform the rituals periodically, offer prayers and sacrifices to the deity on behalf of Umuaro. Besides, he also enjoys the privilege of keeping the agricultural calender of the community. In this capacity, he names and conducts two important events of Umuaro: namely, the festival of Pumpkin Leaves – a ceremony of Purification before plantation and the New Yam Festival or the Harvest Festival which marks the end of the old year and heralds the new year. Ezeulu is also the guardian and custodian of the community in matters affecting the security and other secular problems of the people. Thus, he is invested with vast powers and responsibilities. But in all the matters related to the security and secular issues of Umuaro, Ezeulu is expected to convene the Umuaro Council comprising the elders and the titled men to arrive at a consensus. This is how a system of checks and balances is ensured against possible authoritarian trends. This is in accordance with the Igbo tradition of dualism governing every action – big or small, individual or community, religious or secular, material or spiritual, events of routine or cosmic nature, and finally, human or divine. The Igbo tradition would not trust either human beings or divine powers with absolute authority. Everything in the world of the Igbo is subject to scrutiny and evaluation from time to time. Thus, it is both traditional and modern at the same time.

The novels of Achebe are political with the exception of *No Longer at*

Ease. *Arrow of God* is not only a political novel, but "also a study in the psychology of power." [3] All the characters in the novel – minor or major, natives or Europeans – revolve round Ezeulu.

As the novel opens, Ezeulu, the old Chief Priest, is introduced straining his eyes to look for the new moon so as to keep track of the passing months enabling him to name different events and festivals from time to time throughout the year:

> Whenever Ezeulu considered the immensity of his power over the year and the crops and, therefore, over the people he wondered if it was real. It was true he named the day for the feast of the Pumpkin Leaves and for the New Yam feast; but he did not choose it. He was merely a watchman. His power was no more than the power of a child over a goat that was said to be his. As long as the goat was alive it could be his; he would find it food and take care of it. But the day it was slaughtered he would know soon enough who the real owner was. No! the Chief Priest of Ulu was more than that, must be more than that. If he should refuse to name the day there would be no festival – no planting and no reaping. But could he refuse? No Chief Priest had ever refused. So it could not be done. He would not dare. (3)

Ezeulu was stung to anger by this as though his enemy had spoken it.

> 'Take away that word dare,' he replied to this enemy. 'Yes I say take it away. No man in all Umuaro can stand up and say that I dare not. The woman who will bear the man who will say it has not been born yet.'
>
> But this rebuke brought only momentary satisfaction. His mind never content with shallow satisfactions crept again to the brinks of knowing. What kind of power was it if it would never be used? Better to say that it was not there, that it was no more than the power in the anus of the proud dog who sought to put out a furnace with his puny fart. (3-4)

It is a human tendency, rather a psychological phenomenon from infancy onwards to do a forbidden thing. A child's fascination to touch and feel fire; a young man's/woman's love for adventure; and Eve's temptation to eat the forbidden fruit (Satan's influence apart) – all constitute a subconscious streak of rebellion against the conventional code. The temptation in all these matters is irresistible. That his role is no more than of 'a watchman' is unacceptable to Ezeulu. The word 'dare' hurled at him as though by an 'enemy' is in the nature of a challenge to the ambitious and egocentric priest. He indulges in a sort of internal monologue as to the nature and reality of power vested in him. He wonders what use is power if it is only superficial, elusive and cannot be exercised. If this is what power means, he would rather not have it at all. Ezeulu is caught up in this dilemma and tension arising out of the limitations and the absoluteness of power. The rest of the novel, I feel, is a natural corollary of power-game influencing various characters and incidents in the novel at different stages. Ezeulu's equation with his deity Ulu, the community of Umuaro including his well-wishers and rivals, Captain Winterbottom and Tony Clarke, the interrelatedness between the individual and community in the context of the Igbo tradition, are all power-oriented. This chapter attempts to study and examine these power relations which seem to me to be seminal to the understanding of the novel.

II

Before Ezeulu's relationship with Ulu is examined, it is imperative to shed light on the Igbo pantheon of gods, godhood, the role, place and significance of gods. Differentiating between the gods of Umuaro and the gods in the Judaeo-Christian world, Chidi Amuta observes:

> while in the Judaeo-Christian world view, deity precedes human existence: in the world of Umuaro, man creates god to serve his social and economic needs . . . the supreme deity, Ulu, is a 'synthetic' deity, fashioned by the peoples of six villages that make up Umuaro to meet their need for collective security against the ravages of slave traders.[4]

Gods of Umuaro created as they are by man, are at his mercy for their sustained survival. They face the threat of disintegration when they fail to serve the purpose for which they are intended. Lyn Innes reinforces the same idea when she says: "The making and allocating of gods by man is further emphasized in Ezeulu's story of how the villagers of Okperi gave the Umuaroans their deities – their Udo and their Ogwugulu."[5]

The works of Hamidou Kane, Worku, Sembene Ousmane, Yambo Ouloguuem and Armah also present a similar portrayal of godhood. Discussing the works of these writers, Soyinka comments:

> When gods die – that is, fall to pieces – the carver is summoned and a new god comes into life. The old is discarded, left to rot in the . . . bush and eaten by termites. In literature the writer aids the process

> of desuetude by acting as the termite or by ignoring the old deity and creating new ones. . . . In African literature this is an organic step; the gods themselves, unlike the gods of Islam and Christianity are already prone to secularism; they cannot escape their history. The writer does little more than stretch that history into tangible and affective reality at whatever point of history he chooses to bring alive. [6]

This is, precisely, what Achebe chooses to do in *Arrow of God*. But Soyinka is sore with Achebe for his "skimpy" treatment of gods and godhood in the novel. Achebe's portrayal and parading of gods in a public appearance is almost parallel to what Soyinka seeks to infer from various African writers dealing with the issue of gods and godhood. In *Arrow of God*, the New Yam Festival provides an opportunity for the public appearance of smaller gods who

> rode into the market place on the heads or shoulders of their custodians, danced round and then stood side by side at the entrance to the shrine of Ulu. Some of them would be very old, nearing the time when their power would be transferred to new carvings and they would be cast aside; and some would have been made only the other day. The very old ones carried face marks like the men who made them, in the days before Ezeulu's grandfather proscribed the custom. At last year's festival only three of these ancients were left. Perhaps this year one or two more would disappear, following the men who made them in their own image and departed long ago. The festival thus brought gods and men together in one crowd. It was the only assembly in Umuaro in which a man might look to his right and find his neighbour and look to his left and see a god standing there. (202)

Commenting on this passage, Soyinka remarks: "The passage sings the dirge, not merely of the gods of Umauro but of godhood itself." [7] He regrets further "the god can initiate nothing, it seems; his role is that of an executor of decisions already taken." [8] Soyinka, obviously, cannot reconcile himself to the fact that "Ezeulu, not Ulu, is cast as the summation of the life-force of Umuaro; without him, the god is reduced to an empty shell." [9] Soyinka's interpretation of god and godhood seems to be orthodox and cannot be applied to what Achebe tries to make of deities in *Arrow of God*. According to Achebe, gods in the context of the Igbo pantheon are anthropomorphous. M.M. Mahood also seems to endorse this view when she says, "Ulu is an anthropomorphous god, who has had a beginning and will one day have an end. . . . the lesser gods of Umuaro . . . are brought out head-high at the New Yam Festival." [10] Thus, according to Satyanarain Singh, God in the novel is de-mystified and brought right into the midst of the people's struggles with the creation of Ulu as the guardian deity of Umuaro. [11]

Nwaka, the "owner of words," knows all about the history of Ulu, his anthropomorphous nature and how the priesthood was served in a platter, as it were, to the weakest among the six villages when the deity was installed. Moreover, in the world of the Igbo, "the divine is an expression or an agent of the human." [12] Ezidemili, the Priest of Idemili, and Nwaka are also aware that their deity had been there from the beginning unlike Ulu who is dated. The rivalry between Nwaka and Ezeulu is dramatised throughout the novel. The former tells his loyal followers of Umuaro *in camera* that Ulu has already outlived his utility in the context of the colonial administration. He says, "If a man says yes his *Chi* also says yes. And we have all heard how the people of Aninta dealt with their deity when he failed them. Did they not carry him to the boundary between them and their neighbours and set fire on him?" (28) And this happens in the early part of the novel in chapter two itself. Thus the fate of Ulu is similar to the ill-fated deity of Aninta. The sword of Damocles, as it were, hangs over his head threatening his existence and survival. In such a situation, "no one, not even a god, is safe from criticism, there are always other people, other gods, ready to supplant their predecessors in their shifting, sceptical Igbo communities." [13] Achebe seems to be of the view that "all gods reside in Blake's phrase, in the human breast." [14]

Thus, the novelist sets the tone and tenor of the novel in terms of the limitation of Ulu and the formidable opposition to him by his rival deity, Idemil and the rivalry between Ezeulu and Nwaka for the supremacy of the clan. *Arrow of God*, thus, deals with "complex relationships and rivalries, the jealous concern for status which influences almost every social contact and Ezeulu is surrounded by a whole web of conflicts and rivalries." [15]

Nwaka is very wealthy, influential and he has won the highest number of titles in Umuaro. He is a famous wrestler and an impressive speaker called "the owner of words." Besides, he has his "flute-player" in Ezedemili. Ezeulu cannot boast of such advantages. But, as the Chief Priest, he claims to be an intermediary between the human and the spirit world. He is both "Known and Unknowable at the same time." (132) "The left half of his body—from forehead to toes—was painted with white chalk" (70) to emphasize the spirit side of his being. Whenever

Ezeulu is confronted with a crisis, he takes recourse either to his "unknowable" aspect of his personality or threatens to laugh as though to mystify the complex issues further.

Ezeulu is alive to the fact that the white man "had not come for a short visit but to build a house and live." (45) The prophecy of the Oracles that he "had come to take over the land and rule" (42) enhances his responsibility to tackle a situation which the ancestors had not imagined. For Ezeulu, "the new religion was like a leper" (42) and the presence of the white man is likened to a "disease that has never been seen before" and which, obviously, "cannot be cured with everyday herbs." (133)

Ezeulu is required to stand upto this sensitive situation and guide the destiny of Umuaro. On the one hand, he is subject to formidable opposition from within and on the other, he has to confront colonial administration ruling the country from the neighbouring Okperi. The quarrel with Okperi over a piece of land brings in Winterbottom, the District Officer, on the scene. Heads roll on both sides in this war. Consequently, "the exercise of judicial coercion and violence belongs solely to the colonial regime" [16] thereafter. The war comes to an abrupt end with the interference of Winterbottom. Ezeulu testifies before the white man against his clan. The disputed land is awarded to Okperi. The white man breaks all the guns of Umuaro in full view of the people except three which he carries to the headquarters for display in his office. Winterbottom has learnt a few Igbo words and is fond of using them frequently. Referring to the guns, he tells Tony Clarke that Winter bottom is named *otijiegbe* by the natives which meant "Breaker of Guns." According to him, Ezeulu was

> a kind of priest-king in Umuaro—witnessed against his own people. I have not found out what it was, but I think he must have had some pretty fierce tabu working on him. But he was a most impressive figure of a man. He was very light in complexion, almost red. One finds people like that now and again among the Ibos. I have a theory that the Ibos in the distant past assimilated a small non-negroid tribe of the same complexion as the Red Indians. (38)

Ezeulu sends his son, Oduche, to the white man's school wanting him to be his 'eye' there and learn the wisdom and secrets of the white man. He is aware of the fact that "there is no escape from the white man." (84) Besides, "the white man, the new religion, the soldiers, the new road—are all part of the same thing. The white man has a gun, a matchet, a bow and carries fire in his mouth. He does not fight with one weapon alone." (85)

However, Ezeulu's intention to test his 'power' is ridden with dangerous potentialities. He "has within him undoubted authoritarian urges at odds with the republican outlook of the people." [17] It is an aggressive individualistic trait which works against the interests of the community. A fine balance is always maintained between the individual and the community in the Igbo tradition – a thing which is nearly alien to the Western world. Achebe's essay entitled "The Nature of the Individual and his Fulfilment" [18] provides an excellent analysis of this problem.

Achebe concedes that the Igbos "are second to none in their respect of the individual personality." [19] However, this individualism is subject to certain limitations. For instance, a sort of democratic obligation, which is an essential feature of the Igbo tradition, "subordinates the person to the group in practical social matters" and secondly, "a moral taboo . . . sets a barrier to personal ambition." [20] Despite Ezeulu's concern for and commitment to his clan, he cannot bring himself to subordinate to his community in its larger interests. He has a tendency to place himself above his community. Moreover, Ezeulu has an inkling to flout the 'moral taboo' which seeks to restrict unbridled "personal ambition."

Nwaka never spares Ezeulu whenever he has an occasion to attack the latter – in the matter of Ezeulu's alleged alliance with the white man; on the issue of sending his son to the white man's school; and Ezeulu's disapproval of war on Okperi. Nwaka accuses Ezeulu on several grounds: "The man who carries a deity is not a king. He is there to perform his god's ritual and to carry sacrifice to him. . . . He is a man of ambition; he wants to be king, priest, diviner, all." (27)

Nwaka, undoubtedly, is guided by a sense of personal grouse, jealousy and ill-will for Ezeulu in his accusations. Yet, it is difficult to deny the element of reality in his assessment of Ezeulu's character.

Of all the persons, Akukalia whose language never wandered far from "kill and despoil" (17) is picked as an emissary of Umuaro to go to Okeperi wanting the Okperians to choose between "war and peace." Akukalia's mother hailed from Okeperi. Despite the ominous nature of Akukalia's mission, he is treated by a kinsman of his mother with a lot of affection. He is addressed as "son of our daughter." Akukalia reciprocates in the same fashion calling his mother's kinsman "father of my mother." (23) For the Igbos, "marriage and parenthood are never private concerns." Obika marries, and his bride is regarded by Ezeulu's two surviving wives and all his children as "their new wife." [21] Thus, there is a sense of the community and reciprocity governing human relations at various levels in the pre-literate African societies. M.M. Mahood says: "the community of Umuaro has continuity as well as cohesion." [22]

III

Achebe juxtaposes the highly individualistic and hierarchial group of five Europeans stationed at the Government Hill of Okperi with the harmonious and warm African community of Umuaro albeit its dissensions and rivalries. Of the five Europeans, Captain Winterbottom is a first generation colonial administrator with the rank of a District Officer. The next in the line-up is Tony Clarke, a second generation colonial administrator. He is a young man and Assistant District Officer. Wright is a Public Works Department man engaged in a road-building activity. The other two are: Roberts and Wade, Police Officers and mentioned as a passing reference in the novel. The character of Winterbottom is portrayed with fun and sarcasm. He is not prepared to credit the natives with any human trait. For him, the natives are 'liars,' 'tyrants' with an 'elemental cruelty' about them. Referring to the natives, he says:

> like children they are great liars. They don't lie simply to get out of trouble. Sometimes they would spoil a good cause by a pointless lie. (38)

> They all manage to turn themselves into little tyrants over their own people. It seems to be a trait in the character of the negro. (107)

and "Winterbottom could only put it down to cruelty of a kind which Africa alone produced. It was this elemental cruelty in the psychological make-up of the native that [he] . . . found so difficult to understand." (58) Captain Winterbottom here refers to corruption and acts of cruelty indulged in by a Warrant Chief appointed by him for Okperi and he generalises these elements of a native individual. Referring to the burial of the living afflicted with abnormal bodily swellings and the like, Winterbottom expresses his nauseating feelings about the Africans: "a man buried alive upto his neck with a piece of roast Yam on his head to attract vultures." (36) Winterbottom can never see the better and finer aspects of the life of the natives. Hence, "his strong belief in the value of the British mission in Africa." (30) The road builder Wright is worse still. For him, the natives are no better than animals. According to him, they are "as loyal as pet dogs." (76)

Captain Winterbottom is obsessed with his civilizing mission in Nigeria. He is an heir to George Allen, the D.C. of *Things Fall Apart* and the author of *The Pacification of the Primitive Tribes of the Lower Niger.* But, poor Winterbottom has his own tale of woe in his personal life. His junior by three years is promoted and placed above him as a Senior District Officer. His wife eloped with a smart guy as he was busy fighting for his "tribal god" [23] (the British Empire) in Cameroon against Germans. In spite of his long innings of fifteen years in Nigeria, the African climate, the rituals and the customs continue to torment him. While Clarke is of the view that the Captain is "a man of high principles, something of a missionary," Wright regrets that he "is too serious to sleep with native women." (103) Captain Winterbottom's sense of contempt is not confined to the climate and inhabitants of Africa alone. When he finds it difficult to eat a hard piece of chicken, he curses the "damned native birds!" (107)

The European group of five persons are highly barricaded by hierarchy and protocol. Wright, Roberts and Wade are "supposed to be beneath the notice of the Political Officers." (100) Winterbottom cuts into the talk of Clarke when the latter calls George Allen 'a missionary,' and describes his book as 'smug.' While both Wright and Clarke heckle and mock Winterbottom in his absence, the latter (C.W.) hurls abuses at the fellow colonial officers of the headquarters. Clarke is jealous of the sex life of Wright. Winterbottom bars Wright from the European Club. Thus, Achebe exposes the hypocrisy and meanness of those engaged in the civilizing mission of Africa. *Arrow of God*, thus, is a fitting reply to the racism of both Joseph Conrad and Joyce Cary.

IV

The white man has broken the guns of Umuaro sending signals to the natives about his might and brute force. Abame was already wiped out in *Things Fall Apart* itself to avenge the killing of one Macdonald. People are quick to understand the menacing presence of the white man and are scared of him. With the result, "no one spoke of war any more in these days of the white man." (141)

Oduche, Ezeulu's son, instead of learning the white man's wisdom and secrets, boxes in the royal python worshipped by Ezedemili and Nwaka The royal python is worshipped as Father. Ezeulu is disturbed at this. Both Akuebue and Edogo disapprove the action of Ezeulu in sending Oduche to the white man's religion. Edogo complains to Akuebue about his father's intentions and says: "A man should hold his compound together, not plant dissension among his children." (126) He suspects that his father seems to be grooming Nwafo for the priesthood.

Ezeulu seems to be guided by more than one reason in sending Oduche to the white man's school. In the first place, he hopes that Oduche will be his 'eye' there and report to him about the secrets and wisdom of the white man. This is how he plans to "confront danger before it reached his people" and that "a man must dance the dance prevalent in his time." (189) On being pressed by Akuebue why he has sent his son to the white man's religion, Ezeulu interprets it in terms of "a sacrifice" just as their ancestors had sacrificed a kinsman to make "the great medicine which they called Ulu." (134) Aluebue is stunned at this revelation which Ezeulu shares with him in confidence.

Akuebue is worried that Ezeulu has already alienated himself from the clan by his evidence against it before the white man and in the matter of sending his son to the new religion. He cautions him not to indulge in such things at least in future. He says: "We did many things wrong in the past, but we should not therefore go on doing the same today. We now know what we did wrong, so we can put it right again. We know where this rain began to fall on us." (132) The image of rain is used recurrently by Achebe both in his fiction and non-fictional writings. Achebe would like his people to look back into their past and learn the right lessons from it so as to guard themselves well in future. In other words, he uses the 'rain' imagery to remind them of what colonialism had done to them in terms of their values, culture and above all, dignity.

Time and again Ezeulu harps on the issue of fighting 'a war of blame' against Okperi and how he was overruled in this matter. But Akuebue argues vehemently to convince him that Ezeulu was wrong in giving evidence against the clan. He says: "Umuaro will always say that you betrayed them before the white man. And they will say that you are betraying them again today by sending your son to join in desecrating the land." (131) Ezeulu seems to be disturbed by this criticism all the more as it has come home to him neither from an enemy, nor from a stranger but from Akuebue who knows Ezeulu better than his children and his wives. Ezeulu feels he is stripped of all his defences at once. He takes recourse to the spirit side of his being and says: "I can see things where other men are blind. That is why I am Known and at the same time I am Unknowable." (132) Akuebue is not convinced by the strange logic, rather the irrationality behind Ezeulu's utterances. Realizing this Ezeulu threatens to laugh and bursts into laughter causing panic in his friend. This testifies to the streak of insanity in Ezeulu.

Soon after this, a messenger of the white man arrives with summons from Winterbottom wanting Ezeulu to see him the following morning at Okperi. Ezeulu is hurt by the insolent behaviour of the messenger and his message and bursts out: "tell your white man that Ezeulu does not leave his hut. If he wants to see me he must come here." (139) Akuebue uses all his skill to defuse a possible ugly scene as both Ezeulu and Obika are enraged. Ezeulu convenes the Umuaro Council to inform it about the summons from the white man. He expects the Council to come to his rescue and support him in his decision not to comply with the white man's summons. But once again he faces humiliation from Nwaka and his men who accuse him of an alliance with the white man. Ezeulu sets out to Okperi nursing grievances agaginst Umuaro.

Captain Winterbottom is enraged to learn about Ezeulu's misbehaviour with his messenger. His decision to appoint Ezeulu as the Chief of Umuaro is given up. Instead, he signs a warrant of arrest and sends two cops to arrest Ezeulu. He says to his assistant, Clarke: "I won't have my natives thinking they can treat the administration with contempt." (149) Strangely enough, Winterbottom falls sick the following morning needing to be hospitalised in a critical condition. He is rushed to the hospital at Enugu where he remains ailing for more than a month.

On his arrival at Okperi, Ezeulu is detained in the guard room as instructed by Captain Winterbottom. Ezeulu realizes it was a full moon night. As he remains boxed in his cell, Ezeulu reflects on his long span as the Chief Priest for eighteen years. For him the priesthood "gave him a feeling of loss which was both painful and pleasant. He had temporarily lost his status as Chief Priest which was painful; but after eighteen years it was a relief to be without it for a while." (160) Obviously, Ezeulu feels the burden of having been the Chief Priest for so long and all that it entails. Hence, his sense of relief.

Akuebue visits Ezeulu in the latter's cell. The latter says with anguish that the white man who "is in the mouth of death . . . wants a Chief Priest to be sacrificed at his funeral." (167) He is produced before Clarke (who according to Ezeulu, "had little sense") on the fourth day. He feels insulted the way he is treated and asked his name. He rejects bluntly the offer of the white man to him to be the Chief of Umuaro. He says: "Tell the white man that Ezeulu will not be anybody's chief, except Ulu." (175) Clarke is enraged that Ezeulu makes a mockery of the British administration. Following this, Ezeulu's reputation as a man of courage and integrity rises both at Okperi and Umuaro. Ezeulu is satisfied that he has become "even" with the white man. However, Nwaka attributes this action of Ezeulu to the latter's lunacy and pride. He is in white man's custody for thirty-two days and in the process, he has already made "an ass" of the colonial administration. Clarke is intrigued as to how he could keep Ezeulu in custody any longer without valid or justifiable grounds. Hence, Ezeulu is set free.

V

The temptation on the part of Ezeulu to test the nature of his power over seasons and people in Chapter I; the internecine clan rivalries from within in Chapter II; and the powerful presence of the white man in Chapter III and later, are sought to be woven into a complex web by the novelist.

Ezeulu misses two moons due to his incarceration for thirty-two days at Okperi. Consequently, there are two extra Yams which remain unconsumed. Customarily and in accordance with his ritual, he eats only one Yam when he sights the new moon and declares the New Yam Festival after eating the twelfth Yam. Then the harvesting is undertaken. Ezeulu defers the naming of this festival on the ground that no one broke kolanut and offered sacrifices to Ulu during his absence. People are worried as the Yam crop begins to rot in the earth and they remain locked up in the old year itself.

Ezeulu returns home to the accompaniment of a heavy rain and the son of John Nwodika. He resolves to wreak vengeance on Umuaro for his humiliation and betrayal to the white man. On the first night of his detention, he has a dream in which he sees Nwaka challenging him and calling him "the priest of a dead god." (159) His "muscles tingled for the fight" (160) as his "mind twists with rage against the people of Umuaro who have shut him into the box of the white man." [24]

Back home, Ezeulu is given a hero's reception. People of Umuaro visit him in large numbers and express their sense of relief for his safe return. The warmth and affection with which Umuaroans hold him move him immensely. He realizes that his grievances and anger for the clan are not justifiable.

Ogbuefi Ofaka, who is neither a friend nor an enemy of Ezeulu, conveys to him the feelings of Umuaro with a considerable measure of sincerity. He says: "Who else among us could have gone out and wrestled with him [the white man] as you have done?" (188) These words of Ofaka mellow Ezeulu, and his determination to hit his people loses much of its bite and sting.

Ezeulu toys with several alternatives at this stage. He thinks in terms of a possible reconciliation; of "narrowing down the area of conflict"; and "dissolve his resolution" for the present, and "form it again" (191) when the New Yam Festival falls due. In any case, he almost decides to defer the matter of settling his scores with Umuaro. But, precisely at this moment, Ulu barks in his ear to say,

> "Who told you that this was your own fight?" Ezeulu trembled and said nothing, his gaze lowered to the floor.
>
> "I say who told you that this was your own fight to arrange the way it suits you? You want to save your friends who brought you palm wine he-he-he-he-he!" Only the insane could sometimes ap-

> proach the menace and mockery in the laughter of deities – a dry, skeletal laugh. "Beware you do not come between me and my victim or you may receive blows not meant for you! Do you not know what happens when two elephants fight? Go home and sleep and leave me to settle my quarrel with Idemili, whose envy seeks to destroy me so that his python may again come to power. Now you tell me how it concerns you. I say go home and sleep. As for me and Idemili we shall fight to the finish; and whoever throws the other down will strip him of his anklet!"
>
> After that there was no more to be said. Who was Ezeulu to tell his deity how to fight the jealous cult of the sacred python? It was a fight of the gods. He was no more than an arrow in the bow of his god. This thought intoxicated Ezeulu like palm wine. (191-92)

'Ulu's voice' is a challenge both to Ulu's rivals as well as to several critics who feel intrigued by it as to its source and significance. Several critics have interpreted 'Ulu's voice' in different ways. According to David Carroll, "Ulu has reasserted his control over the divine half of Ezeulu's ambiguous nature in an unmistakable way, and all doubts and perplexities are resolved. . . . Now the priest becomes once more the remote agent of the supreme god, rather than the representative of the clan." [25]

By choosing to be a god's agent and not a representative of the clan, Ezeulu allows himself to be alienated from his community. Such an alienation sets in the process of his disintegration and his tragedy. Chidi Amuta observes: "His [Ezeulu's] tragedy, then, is essentially one of a basic dislocation between individual action and the demands of a historical imperative requiring collective assertion." [26] Since Ulu is a creation of man, comments Lynn Innes, "One must see Ezeulu's submission to Ulu's authority as if he were a mere arrow in the bow of God, as a violation of the concept of the god as originally created." [27] She says further: "Once Ezeulu sets himself and Ulu apart from and against his community, both lose their primary role and meaning." [28] M.M. Mahood makes a very striking observation when she says: "This intervention of Ulu is of course Ezeulu's surrender to the irrational, to the idols of the den; he abrogates all responsibility and luxuriates in the belief that he is no more than an arrow in the bow of his god. Resentment is exalted into retribution: Vengeance is Ulu's." [29] Ulu's voice, in the opinion of S. Singh, "signifies a break with the secular principle while it forges a link with the fetish beliefs." [30] He comments further psychologising the Chief Priest. "Ezeulu renounces his capacity to think and analyse particularly when the 'revelation' so happily accorded with his own incipient thirst for revenge against Nwaka and Idemili – even if in the process, his own family and most of the ordinary men friendly to Ezeulu get hurt or even destroyed. Passion displaces reason." [31]

Most of these perceptive and insightful comments by all these critics related to Ulu's voice seek to corroborate Ezeulu's own designs for revenge and revolve round a single issue that Ezeulu finds it convenient to take shelter under the spirit side of his being and that he behaves as the helpless agent of his deity, rather than the representative of his clan. This is a valid judgement on Ulu voice. But, the issues involved in Ulu's voice are much more complex and ambivalent. Ezeulu is haunted by his temptation to test his power throughout the novel. It is part of his subconscious to experience what it is in real terms. He is not the one to be satisfied with indirect power just as Captain Winterbottom is disgusted with the kind of Indirect Rule imposed on him from above by those at the Headquarters. Both Ezeulu and Winterbottom make a mockery of the Indirect Rule as envisaged by Lord Lugard for Nigeria. They seek to enjoy power in absolute terms and refuse to share it with others. What Ezeulu attempts is to superimpose his own sense of authority on his deity Ulu so as to lend a greater credibility and authenticity to Ulu's voice. On his way back home following his release from the white man's custody, Ezeulu tells John Nwodika's son in a fit of anger against Umuaro throwing an open challenge to it for a combat. He said: "whoever throws the other will strip him of his anklet." (179) Ulu, who barks in Ezeulu's ear, expresses the same feeling in identical words: "whoever throws the other down will strip him of his anklet!" (192)

The language of Ezeulu and Ulu's voice is the same *verbatim* except the addition of the adverb 'down' and the mark of exclamation in the latter. Ezeulu's sense of "personal power" and "the temptation to constitute himself into an arrow of God" [32] need to be looked at from this power perspective. Lynn Innes maintains that no single perspective can explain the point of view in the novel as it insists "continually on the variety of perspectives, the necessity of considering all possibilities, the constant demand to judge and the difficulty of making decisions." [33] Besides, Ezeulu's bouts of insanity as manifested through his irrational laughter many a time, and the way he says and repeats 'he!' five times as part of Ulu's voice and the subtle historic processes of change at work also contribute considerably to Ulu's voice.

The fatal decision of Ezeulu to defer the naming of the New Yam Festival shocks and stuns all the people of Umuaro. A group of ten elders of the clan – most of them are titled and men of considerable influence – visit Ezeulu and persuade him to eat the Yams and declare the Festival enabling people to carry out harvesting operations. They try to convince

Ezeulu how "certain customs . . . had been altered in the past when they began to work hardship on the people" (209) and that there is a price for any calamity which could be paid by way of a sacrifice to the deity. But Ezeulu's only reply to all this is: "the gods sometimes use us as a whip." (208) Ofaka feels stung by this reply and asks him on "whose side" Ezeulu is – whether he is with the people or against them in their hour of crisis. This is an issue with which most of the writings of Ngugi are concerned.

Ezeulu at last agrees to consult the deity to find a solution to the crisis. His approach to Ulu is very mechanical and he returns from the shrine to inform the elders that there is no response from the deity. Ezeulu's doggedness in his refusal to name the festival is interpreted in several ways by various characters. Ofaka comments that Ezeulu "has caught his mother's madness" so that "he would rather see the six villages ruined rather than eat two Yams." (212) He adds further: "The house he has been planning to pull down has caught fire and saved him the labour." (213) The implication in this statement is that the historical processes of change are already there on the anvil and all that Ezeulu has done is to act as a catalyst in this process. Ofaka argues in the same vein. "A priest like Ezeulu leads a god to ruin himself" or in the reverse, "a god like Ulu leads a priest to ruin himself." (213)

Meanwhile, the ripe crop of Yams begins to rot in the earth. Ezeulu becomes "a public enemy in the eyes of all." (211) His family shares in his guilt and faces hostility from the clan. People no longer care for Ezeulu and shun him. He also realizes how lonely and alienated he has become all of a sudden. Even at this stage, "Beneath all anger in his mind lay a deeper compassion for Umuaro." (219) The sudden and tragic death of Obika, his most favourite son, is like the last straw on the camel's back. The cumulative effect of all these things "left a crack in Ezeulu's mind" so that Ezeulu, in his last days lives "in the haughty splendour of a demented high priest and spared . . . [the] knowledge of the final outcome." (229) "The final outcome" is offering of sacrifices in the form of Yams and other things to the alien god of Christianity in exchange for their harvest and the promised security against the possible wrath of Ulu. The alien god steps in promptly to fill the vacuum created by the exit of the indigenous god and the inexorable laws of changing times. Thereafter, the crops were harvested not in honour of Ulu but "in the name of the son." (230)

John Updike expresses his sense of surprise at the abrupt manner with which Ezeulu's downfall is made possible "in a page or two" by Achebe. The novelist quotes a passage from Updike's letter to him.

> The final developments of *Arrow of God* proved unexpected and, as I think about them, beautifully resonant, tragic and theological. That Ezeulu whom we had seen stand up so invincibly to both Nwaka and Clarke, should be so suddenly vanquished by his own god Ulu and by something harsh and vengeful within himself, and his defeat in a page or two be the fulcrum of a Christian lever upon his people, is an ending few Western novelists would have contrived; having created a hero, they would not let him crumble, nor are they, by and large, as truthful as you in their witness to the cruel reality of process.[34]

True. A Western mind finds it difficult to bring itself to accept such an abrupt fall of an invincible hero like Ezeulu. Achebe explains at length in this article the fundamental and conceptual distinction between a Western and non-Western sensibility in respect of a hero. The Western sensibility visualises a hero in terms of his aristocracy, nobility of character, the tragic flaw, the gradual rise and fall and so on and so forth in the conventional pattern. In contrast, all that the non-western mind looks for or appreciates is not a hero of high rank and status, but a common man, "the human hero"[35] or an anti-hero of the modern times. Besides, a close look at Ezeulu's character since the beginning of the novel and subsequently, convinces one that he is prone to power and that his fall is imminent at any stage in the novel. Besides, he is also cast in a tragic mould.

What Achebe does in this novel is to fictionalise the clan loyalties and political rivalries which began to plague the body politic of the new independent state of Nigeria in the first few years of self-rule. But Achebe chooses not this particular context but the historical sequence of events of the 1920s of the Igboland so as to mirror in greater depth the myths, rituals and traditions of this clan than what is attempted in *Things Fall Apart*. *Arrow of God* successfully drives home the message that "no man however great can win judgement against a clan." The novel is structured on this thematic principle emphasizing that power rests with the group, the community and the society. Any attempt by an individual to tamper with this principle can only be counter-productive and disastrous in the ultimate analysis. This, precisely, is the predicament and the tragedy of the priest in the novel as he fails to strike a rational equation between himself and his deity, and the community.

NOTES

1. Chinua Achebe, *Arrow of God* (London: Heinemann Educational Books, 1964), p. 175.
2. Simon Nnmolim, *The History of Umuchu* (Enugu: Eastern Syndicate Press, 1953).
3. David Carroll, *Chinua Achebe* (London: Macmillan, 1980), p. 123.
4. Chidi Amuta, *The Theory of African Literature* (London: Zed Books, 1989), p. 123.
5. C.L. Innes, *Chinua Achebe*, p. 76.
6. Wole Soyinka, *Myth, Literature and the African World* (Cambridge: Cambridge University Press, 1976), p. 86.
7. *Ibid.*, p. 93.
8. *Ibid.*, p. 95.
9. *Ibid.*, p. 96.
10. M.M. Mahood, "Idols of the Den: Achebe's *Arrow of God*," *Critical Perspectives on Chinua Achebe* (Washington: Three Continent Press, 1978), p. 189.
11. Satyanarain Singh, "The Spiritual in terms of the secular: Achebe's social vision in *Arrow of God*," *Colonial and Neo-Colonial Encounters in Commonwealth Literature* (Mysore: Prasarange University of Mysore, 1983), p. 133.
12. David Carroll, p. 93.
13. *Ibid.*, p. 92.
14. M.M. Mahood, p. 188.
15. C.L. Innes, p. 71.
16. Emmanuel Obiechina, "The Human Dimension of History in *Arrow of God*," *Critical Perspectives on Chinua Achebe*, p. 172.
17. *Ibid.*, p. 174.
18. Chinua Achebe, "The Nature of the Individual and his Fulfilment," *The Colonial and the Neo-Colonial Encounters in Commonwealth Literature*, pp. 205-15.
19. *Ibid.*, pp. 214-15.
20. *Ibid.*, p. 215.
21. M.M. Mahood, p. 181.
22. *Ibid.*, p. 182.
23. *Ibid.*, p. 187.
24. *Ibid.*, p. 196.
25. David Carroll, p. 116.
26. Chidi Amuta, *The Theory of African Literature*, p. 135.

27. C.L. Innes, pp. 79-80.
28. *Ibid.*, p. 79.
29. M.M. Mahood, p. 198.
30. Satyanarain Singh, p. 131.
31. *Ibid.*,
32. C.L. Innes, p. 80.
33. Emmanuel Obiechina, p. 170.
34. As quoted by Achebe in "The Nature of the Individual and his Fulfilment," p. 214.
35. *Ibid.*

Uhuru, Betrayals and Reconciliation
A Grain of Wheat

> We need to talk, to open our hearts to one another, examine them, and then together plan the future we want. [1]

The three novels discussed so far deal with the pre-colonial and colonial phases of Africa. At the superficial level, *A Grain of Wheat* is concerned with the celebrations of Uhuru (independence) in Kenya slated for December 12, 1963. Four days before the celebrations, a group of freedom fighters and Gikonyo, the local Chairman of the Party of Thabai, approach Mugo, the legendary "village hero" (180) wanting him to lead the procession on the historic day and deliver the main speech at Rung'ei in honour of the memory of those killed in the freedom struggle. (Thabai and Rung'ei are the fictional locale of the novel.)

The story proper of the novel relates itself to the events of the four days preceding Uhuru celebrations and terminates with the event. But the time scale (of Ngugi) in the novel moves back and forth fairly frequently taking the reader to the early days of colonialism through the heroic struggles against it by Waiyaki at the beginning of the present century; Harry Thuku in the 1920s; Jomo Kenyatta in the 50s; and finally, Kihika, the fictional leader of the Mau Mau rebellion a little later until the attainment of Uhuru. Besides, a greater part of the story of the novel is narrated through the consciousness of various protagonists.

While *The River Between* attempts to recreate the myths, rituals and traditions of the central Gikuyu land, *Weep Not, Child* fictionalises the Mau Mau rebellion of the 50s. *A Grain of Wheat* sets before itself a much more complex and ambitious framework in terms of its sweeping thematic range so as to cover the national history of Kenya underlining the heroic struggles against colonialism. In other words, the novel recreates the history of Kenya emphasising Ngugi's conviction that "the writer himself lives in, and is shaped by, history." [2] In the process of the delineation of history, the novelist captures the apprehensions and aspirations of the people on the eve of Uhuru. The apprehensions are due to a tradition of betrayal at various stages of the nationalist upsurge inaugurated by Harry Thuku in the 1920s. Ngugi also envisions the hopes of the people at the birth of a new nation – "hand in hand and eager to build a new country, and sing a new song" [3] with a sense of unity and harambee (pulling together) in the post-independence era.

Artistically, *A Grain of Wheat* is Ngugi's best piece of fiction. While writing this novel, Ngugi seems to have been "totally immersed in a world of imagination which is other than his conscious self. At his most intense and creative, the writer is transfigured, he is possessed, he becomes a medium." [4] The novelist delves deep into the psyche of his characters so as to portray them with their perfections and fallibilities; excellences and shortcomings; weaknesses and strength. In other words, the novel is a palpable delineation of human nature under stresses and strains. The world of the novel does not seek to praise sky-high the individual hero or heroes, nor does it attempt to condemn people with a bad patch as downright villains. The novel marks a radical departure from the established tradition in the concept of heroism. The term 'protagonism,' I feel, is more appropriate to Ngugi's sense of heroism. Marginal people, who are never part of the recorded history of a nation, are sought to be given due recognition and are portrayed as makers of the history in the novel.

The complex and contradictory motifs of religion and rebellion; frailty and fallibility in human nature; the burden of alienation and the sense of belonging to the community; the colonial attempts at civilizing a dark continent and the native's search for identity through nationalist struggles; hopes and aspirations of the people at the birth of a new nation; white violence and counter-violence, irony and mimicry; a sense of gloom and of hope – constitute the comprehensive matrix of the novel. This chapter attempts to analyse and examine these issues.

II

Ngugi chooses a Christian myth and a religious framework to depict the violent freedom movement in Kenya. The title of the novel is itself from the Bible:

> Thou fool, that which Thou sowest is not quickened, except it die. And that which thou sowest, thou sowest not that body that shall be, but bare again, it may chance of wheat, of some other grain.
>
> (I *Corinthians* 15:36)

This epigraph appended to the novel is an attempt by St. Paul to answer queries by some Corinthians as to the possibility of the resurrection of the mortal body of Christ. St. Paul hints at the 'potentiality' of the mortal frame to get itself renewed in life for a second coming. But like a sown seed, it has to die first before it can be born again. The image of dying to be born again runs recurrently and is central to the novel. In other words, the alchemy of "rebirth and regeneration" [5] always lies embedded in a dying seed as a strong "potential" only waiting to be born again "through the will of *God*." [6]

Ngugi applies this Christian epigraph to the gory nationalist struggle aganist colonialism. Referring to the matyrdom of Waiyaki during the early phase of this struggle, the novelist observes: "Waiyaki's blood contained within it a seed, a grain, which gave birth to a movement whose main strength thereafter sprang from a bond with the soil." (12) Waiyaki sacrifices his life. But he rises again Phoenix like in the form of a potential and formidable movement. This movement is organically linked to the soil of the people so as to provide succour, strength and inspiration to them in designing and building a new nation corresponding to their aspirations. Emphasising the need for sacrifice by one and all for a national cause, Kihika says:

> I die for you, you die for me, we become a sacrifice for one another. So I can say that you, Karanja, are Christ. I am Christ. Everybody who takes the Oath of Unity to change things in Kenya is a Christ. Christ then is not one person. All those who take up the cross of liberating Kenya are the true Christs for us Kenyan people (95).

According to Govind Naraian Sharma, "Kihika is a true Christ who, through sacrifice, not only justifies himself but also brings about a revolution in the lives of his friends and followers by showing them the way to the spiritual regeneration." [7] Such a spirited defence of Kihika seeks to transcend the limitations of a religious principle so as to cover and embrace a secular pursuit; a social ethic; a national aspiration and a sense of commitment. Obviously, Kihika's sense of religion is not confined to its meaning in an abstraction but it is sought to be applied to a people engaged in a grim battle against colonial forces. Kihika feels stung by a remark made by his friend, Karanja, who reminds Kihika of his own saying that "Jesus had failed." (94) Karanja even wonders whether Kihika is trying to resort to religious revivalism. For a moment, Kihika is nonplussed. But he does not give in to the sarcasm or the logistics of Karanja. He continues to argue forcefully:

> I said he [Christ] had failed because his death did not change anything, it did not make his people find a centre in the cross. All op-

> pressed people have a cross to bear. The Jews refused to carry it and were scattered like dust all over the earth. . . . In Kenya we want deaths which will change things, that is to say, we want true sacrifice. But first we have to be ready to carry the cross. (95)

This passage has several layers of meaning and inferences. It points out categorically that Christ had failed in the Kenyan context. This is a common phenomenon in any colonial situation where the alien religion of Christianity always tended to support an oppressive regime causing hardships to the colonised. Ngugi is of the view that Christianity as an organised institution, paved the way for the coloniser and unhesitatingly supported him in consolidating his position in the colonies. Africans were also taken away from their places as slaves and scattered "all over the earth." Hence, the novelist appeals to the suffering masses the world over "to carry the cross" and bear the burden and take the fire right into the midst of the enemy's camp using the tools of the religion and the sword or the gun which had been used so far by the colonial master.

III

Ngugi's adaptation of the Christian epigraph has social implications and political overtones in the context of the novel. Apart from the religious outfit, the novel hinges on a vital irony which runs as an undercurrent throughout. This element of irony is used to delineate yet another important motif of betrayal. The motif of betrayal, a vital issue in the novel, serves as a lesson to be learnt from the past experiences.

The very name of Mugo has a sense of irony about it. Mugo wa Kabira is the ancient prophet of the Gikuyu land, whose prophecy about the arrival of the white man was ignored by his people. Often, he is referred to as "our village hero." (180) Praising Mugo, Gikonyo says, "Your name and that of Kihika will ever be linked together." (23) Indeed, their names are "linked together" in an ironic sense since the former betrays the latter to the white man. Mugo lived his life avoiding conflicts and involvements. But, once Kihika enters his life, he feels drawn into what he has avoided carefully. He finds himself caught up in a situation of making a "moral choice," [8] either to align himself with Kihika and all that the latter represents or move to the side of the coloniser. Unfortunately, Mugo "makes the wrong choice without knowing he has made a moral choice, without realizing the impact of such a choice. . . . Mugo realizes too late that by giving up Kihika he has betrayed his own humanity." [9] In other words, Mugo is not well prepared either for a serious involvement or to exercise a crucial choice.

When Mugo refuses to play the leading role at the Uhuru celebrations, Wambui feels unhappy about it and says, "Independence Day withhout him [Mugo] would be stale; he is Kihika born again." (180) The image of being "born again," the recurrent motif in the novel, is used here ironically. On another occasion, Gikonyo showers his compliments on Mugo and adds: "You have a great heart. It is people like you who ought to have been the first to taste the fruits of independece." (68) The novel abounds in instances like these. The novelist maintains suspense about Mugo as a "reticent hermit" almost until the latter's confession towards the end of the novel.

The element of betrayal in the context of the novel arises out of harassment and torture to which the prisoners (freedom fighters) are subjected in various detention camps. Gatu is a lively detainee who keeps entertaining the fellow detainees with his sense of humour and his ability to narrate tales and crack jokes bordering on ribaldry. Gikonyo's confession of the Mau-Mau Oath is an act of betrayal. Like most other detainees, he had been demoralised by the cold-blooded murder of Gatu. Gikonyo's betrayal is also influenced by his desire to join his Mumbi "who appeared so pure, an incorruptible reality in a world of changing shadows. Her purity crushed him, . . . " Gikonyo returns home only to be disillusioned. Mumbi has a child by Karanja during his absence. Karanja also admits his oath and betrays his friend's wife. It is extremely painful to Gikonyo. He says: "there is nothing so painful as finding that a friend, or a man you always trusted, has betrayed you." (122) Gikonyo seeks to find his identity and fulfilment through his involvement in love with Mumbi. He feels disgusted as he finds all round nothing but betrayal. He shifts the image of 'purity' to Mugo, little realizing that Mugo is no angel. According to him, "Mugo's purity, Mumbi's unfaithfulness, everything had conspired to undermine his manhood." (123) But the fact is no one is pure in the world of adulterated relationships as delineated in the novel.

IV

Feminine principle is yet another significant motif in the novel. Gikonyo finds his fulfilment only through his love for Mumbi. The image of Mumbi is that of a benevolent mother, an understanding companion and a lovable personality. She is the source of inspiration and encouragement to Gikonyo and others. According to G.N. Sharma, she is "an angelic figure . . . generous, forgiving and compassionate, an embodiment of Ngugi's humane vision." [10]

It is through his communion with her that Gikonyo begins to taste and register success in life. His involvement with her shows him the way, gives a sense of 'clarity' to his otherwise mundane existence and provides a "meaning" to his life. Gikonyo recollects how the magic touch of hers has transformed him from an ordinary, commonplace position to a man of worth and eminence. Looking back at his brief married life, Gikonyo feels how "it [the magic touch of Mumbi] was all important . . . I discovered . . . I had made a covenant with God to be happy . . . I felt whole, renewed." (99) This magic touch and the sacred communion between the two has a creative force about it so that it "was like being born again." (99) During the period of his detention, he held on to the image of Mumbi beckoning him, and "awakening in him emotions almost cracked by physical hardships and pains of waiting." (105)

Karanja is also very much fascinated by the charming beauty of Mumbi. He craves for her love and proposes to her several times. It is always a close race between himself and Gikonyo for Mumbi's love. He could never surmise how she falls to Gikonyo whom he is not prepared to consider as a "serious rival" in love. He knows Gikonyo is "without wit or any suavity." (92) But strange and mysterious are the ways of lovers. Mumbi shows her preference for the ordinary and less known Gikonyo to the more resourceful and wealthy Karanja.

It was a weak moment that impelled her to submit herself to Karnaja's advances. However, her momentary frailty fills her with self-flagellation and anger so that she throws his shoe at him. She says: "When I woke and realized fully what had happened, I became cold. . . . I could see he was laughing at me with triumph. I took one of his shoes and I threw it at him." (151) Ironically enough, her joyous euphoria – on hearing the news of her husband's release from Karanja – turns into a traumatic experience.

It is Mumbi who unwittingly exacts the truth of Mugo's betrayal of Kihika by her own candid and forthright admission of her strained conjugal relationship with her husband. Mumbi "had trusted him [Mugo] and confided in him. This simple trust had forced him to tell her the truth." (234) G.N. Sharma observes: "The open honesty with which she told her own story to Mugo made him ashamed of his morbid secretiveness." [11] Wambui, Warui and Gikonyo fail to persuade Mugo to lead the procession and do the main speech at the Uhuru celebrations. Finally, this mission is entrusted to Mumbi. She relishes it hoping to do the magic with Mugo and succeed where others have failed. She tells herself: "What if she succeeded where he [Gikonyo] had failed? The thought thrilled her; she contemplated the mission with satisfaction." (182) Although she fails to convince Mugo about her mission, her failure is more than compensated as she not only succeeds in getting the truth of Mugo's betrayal, but she is also largely responsible for the presence of Mugo on the dais to make the startling and stunning confession in full view of people at the Uhuru celebrations. Even though Mumbi keeps Mugo's guilt a heavily guarded secret, the latter is conscious that it is no longer a secret. This awareness prompts Mugo to walk to the dais as a hero as though to undo himself rather than suffer for life the burden and the agony of a guilt-conscience. Thus, Mumbi does succeed in her mission, ironically though, more than she or any other person anticipated.

Mumbi belongs to the strong breed of Ngugi women with an inherent ability to rise to any occasion and stand upto any adverse situation. She nearly challenges Gikonyo when the latter pushes around her child crudely. She says: "What sort of a man do you call yourself? Have you no manly courage to touch me? Why do you turn a coward's anger on a child, a little child." (168) Mumbi "seethed like a river that has broken the dam." (168) She is not the one to bear or tolerate any humiliation. When she realizes that Gikonyo begins to behave unreasonably with her, she approaches Mugo expecting him to sort out the problem of her conjugal relationship. Not many women can be expected to share the secret of their conjugal relations with others – men in particular. When Gikonyo goes beyond a limit in insulting her, she walks out of the 'tomb,' the place of her husband with her pride and dignity in tact. She is determined "not to let Gikonyo think her lonely and miserable." (182) She would never allow him to treat her as "an orphan."

V

Who is the hero of *A Grain of Wheat?* It is difficult to answer this question as there are a number of protagonists in the novel. Each one of them is invested with a certain measure of heroism. Opinion among the critics is also divided on this issue. For some, it is Mugo, while some others look upon Kihika, Mumbi and Gikonyo as heroes. Mugo alone is referred to as "our village hero" in the novel. Mumbi's portrayal is brilliantly done and she largely influences both people and events in the novel. Kihika as the leader of the Freedom Struggle has his own share of heroism. Mugo is almost at the centre stage of action in the novel. Moreover, the history of Kenya and the struggle for freedom occupy as much space and importance as any individual character in the novel. It is significant to note that Ngugi delineates the history of Kenya as a "living reality" through "the consciousness of"[12] his characters. According to Gakwandi, *A Grain of Wheat* "is a creative interpretation of national history in a favourable light."[13]

Ngugi's concept of heroism is different from its conventional sense. He does not project an individual character as a hero as he does not believe in individual heroism. The fictional corpus of Ngugi is committed to protagonism. A unique feature of the novel is that "different characters are linked with one another socially and psychically." [14]

Ngugi seems to have laid the foundation for his concept of multiple protagonism in his very first novel, *Weep Not, Child*. Although the focus of attention in this novel is on Njoroje, his two brothers, Kori and Boro, his father, Ngotho, Mwihaki, the daughter of Jocob, and Njoroje's two mothers—are all prominently portrayed in the novel. Similarly, Muthoni and Nyambura influence the events in *The River Between* as much as Waiyaki. *Petals of Blood* has four major protagonists in Abdulla, Wanja, Munira and Karega and each one of them is endowed with a measure of heroism. The real claims of heroism need to be judged by the "test" of "how long [one] can endure hardship" (211) in a given situation. Although individuals are important and are capable of influencing events and making history, it is only their collective endeavours and struggles in a spirit of harambee, that can provide a meaningful direction and an impetus to the sense of history of a people. Ngugi's protagonists are collectively involved in this process in the novel. They are like cogs in the wheel of history—both in its making and its onward march.

Ali Mazuri pleads for a thorough revision of the very concept of "immaculate hero and damned villain" [15] and also a nation's "martyrology." [16] The concept of protagonism is essentially collectivist in Ngugi's fiction. The portrayal of various protagonists in *A Grain of Wheat* needs to be discussed in terms of their distinct peculiar circumstances and their sense of identity with the community. It is in this context that various protagonists—Warui, Wambui, General R. Lt. Koina, Gatu, Gikonyo, Kihika and Mugo are discussed. All these are rural people.

"Warui's life was . . . the story of the movement"; (18) which itself came into being imperceptibly as soon as the prophecy of Mugo wa Kabira about the arrival of "a people with clothes like the butterflies" (10) became a reality. Warui is the living symbol, an important witness and an active participant in the 1923 procession against the arrest of Harry Thuku and in a similar upsurge against the imprisonment of Jomo Kenyatta and others in 1952. It is only in the fitness of things that he is given a place of prominence at the Uhuru celebrations of Dec. 12, 1963. It is an honour to a rural individual peasant who represents the collective conscience of the rural peasantry of Kenya.

Wambui is not as old as Warui. She is an active participant in the Movement during the Emergency in Kenya. She is something like a "courier" of the modern Liberationist struggles entrusted with the job of carrying messages to and from the forest. Once she "carried a pistol tied to her thighs near the groin." (19) She was interrogated and searched by a homeguard. As the fellow was about to touch the vital spot, she screamed and teased the fellow saying, "I'll lift the clothes and you can have a look at your mother, it is so aged, and see what gain it'll bring you for the rest of your life." (19-20) She made a gesture to lift her clothes, but the fellow leaves her alone and she is let off. Wambui is assigned the role of a judge to try Mugo for the latter's betrayal of Kihika. She is of the view that they "should not have tried him." (243) But, nevertheless, she feels the need "to sweep the room" and "light the fire" as she realizes how "dirt can so quickly collect in a clean hut." (243) Ngugi fulfils his commitment of historicizing marginal men and women as represented by Warui and Wambui.

Koina was conscripted as a cook during the Second World War. He is fiercely independent and bold. After the War, he worked in a white man's shoe factory. When he demanded better wages, a decent house and a car, he was fired. It sobered him a little. Then, he joined Dr. Lynd as a house-boy. She is a spinster but lives in a house which is like a mansion. Her "dog had its own room in the house, with a bed and sheets and blankets!" while most of his fellow countrymen went without a proper roof over their heads. He thought all about this, took the Oath to join the Kenya Land and Freedom Army and became its lieutenant. He is propelled by a passion to drive away "the likes of Dr. Lynd and her dogs from Kenya, a blackman's country." He led two of his colleagues and stormed into Dr. Lynd's home, snatched her two guns and a pistol, and left the place after gang-raping her with vengeance. He also killed her dog with his panga and said, "Let me never see you again in this country." But to his shock, Dr Lynd and her dog (another one) continued to live in the post-independence Kenya as though to mock at the blackman's sense of independence. General R. and he had been in the forest for seven years. He plays an important part at the Uhuru celebrations next to General R.

It is General R. (Russia) under whose direction the celebrations of Uhuru are conducted at Rung'ei. He is obliged to deliver the main speech in place of Mugo. He evolves his own theory of violence and advocates the need for its use in a colonial situation. According to Frantz Fanon, the 'race' dimension is a significant factor in addition to the class-conflict in a revolutionary struggle. General R. like Fanon, lends legitimacy to violence against the oppressor, General R. justifies why they "killed and split blood." He says:

> He who was not on our side, was against us. That is why we killed our black brothers. Because, inside, they were whitemen. And I know even now this war is not ended. We get Uhuru today. But what's the meaning of "Uhuru"? It is contained in the name of our

> Movement: Land and Freedom....
>
> We want a Kenya built on the heroic tradition of resistance of our people. We must revere our heroes and punish traitors and collaborators with the colonial enemy. (221)

General R. is hardened because of his parents, his harrowing experiences of the white man's war, his own underground life in the forest for seven long years. He is on the look out for a sacrifice as part of the Uhuru celebrations. Consequent upon the betrayal of Kihika as confessed by Mugo himself, General pronounced: "The trial will be held tonight . . . your deeds alone will condemn you." (238) Gatu is a detainee in a detention camp. He is probably the most lively character (next to Mumbi) in the novel. He provides fun and laughter in the midst of irony and suspense, tension and violence which are built into the novel. His gruesome murder in cold-blood casts 'a spell of gloom on' the fellow detainees evoking a sense of the macabre on the one hand and empathy on the other. Commenting on this gloomy atmosphere in the novel, Gakwandi observes: "there is a sadness in the novel which makes almost an unrelieved chronicle of pain and suffering." [17] Gatu's sense of the history of the peoples of the world in relation to their liberation struggles in India, America, Russia and Africa is tremendous. His endless narration of stories marked by fantasy and fun and his sense of performance while telling them used to relieve the fellow detainees from their monotony, alienation and disgust.

He joined the Movement fairly early in life. His unflinching faith in it used to inspire the fresh oath seekers to whom he would administer the Oath. He would take the beating and bear the torture like a funeral ram. Often he would be confined in a cell alone because of his skill in "mimicking the English voices and miming their features." (108) Gatu becomes the symbol of the collective resistance to colonialism.

Gatu is a loner in the world without anybody whom he could claim to be his kith and kin. Yet his sense of the community is much more than those who are privileged to enjoy the warmth, comforts and the love of a family life. It was also possible for him "to laugh at himself and others." (111) He was taken away one evening, tortured and hanged in his cell. The death of Gatu thoroughly demoralises the fellow detainees. This unnerves and unsettles Gikonyo who admits his Mau-Mau oath. Gatu's death underlines "the tension between hope and human weakness." [18]

Gikonyo has in him the potentialities of a capitalist. He has a farm-plot of five acres, a shop at Rung'ei and a lorry. On top of it all, he is the local Chairman of the Movement. He achieves all these within four years of his release from detention. The key to his success is due to a sense of application and hard work. He is aware of and very frank about the weak side of his personality. He tells Mugo praising the latter while conceding his own frailty: "I would have sold Kenya to the white man to buy my own freedom." (68) He says further "you have a great heart." (68) It was again Gikonyo who pays tributes to Mugo on the latter's confession of his guilt in public.

> 'He was a brave man, inside,' he said. 'He stood before much honour, praises were heaped on him. He would have become a Chief. Tell me another person who would have exposed his soul for all the eyes to peck at.' He paused and let his eyes linger on Mumbi. Then he looked away and said, 'Remember that few people in that meeting are fit to lift a stone against that man. Not unless I-we-too-in turn open our hearts naked for the world to look at.' (233-34)

Gikonyo's assessment of the heroic streak in Mugo's character is highly incisive and discerning. It points out the need to indulge in self-introspection by one and all to know their weaknesses and limitations.

Mugo is the most complex character in the novel. He is a fascinating person and a great betrayer at the same time. The novel in a way is a study in human nature and human psychology attempted through the psyche of Mugo. Peter Nazareth's comment that the novel has a "psychological subtext" [19] is very appropriate as applied to Mugo. His attempt to wriggle himself out of a tension between his inescapable reality of loneliness and his need to return to the community—is sought to be dramatised by the novelist. According to Robson, Mugo is often "in a state of limbo, poised between the several different images he possesses—the hero, the sufferer, the betrayer, the hermit." [20] This, precisely, is the complex nature of Mugo's personality. On the one hand, he consciously attempts to be free from any involvements with others. On the other hand, he craves for the company of somebody or the other.

Mugo seems to be haunted by a desire "to kill" by strangling with his strong arms. He relishes the image of his attempt to strangle his aunt. The details of the same make one sit up and think what sort of man Mugo is:

> He would get her by the neck, strangle her with his naked hands. Give me the strength; give me the strength, God. He watched her struggle, like a fly in a spider's hands; her muffled groans and cries for mercy reached his ears. He would press harder, make her feel the power in his man's hands. Blood rushed to his finger-tips, he was breathless, acutely fascinated by the audacity and daring of his

own action. (8)

He tells Mumbi that he strangled her brother, Kihika. This is a distortion of the fact. May be he wanted to strangle. He threatens to strangle Mumbi too and he nearly strangles her. After he shares the secret of Kihika's betrayal by him to the white man with her, he becomes hysterical and speaks incoherently, and in a flash jumps at her giving her no chance to escape. She is terrified as he "closed in on her, one hand on her mouth, the other searching her throat. She panted and whimpered horribly." (186) But Mugo comes to his senses soon and releases her from his grip.

Mugo is haunted by the burden of his guilt. Whenever anybody looks at him, he feels 'fixed' and naked. He could not stand the anamoly of being treated as the village hero. Like Gatu, he bears his torture during his detention stoically. Unlike his fellow detainess, he has never taken any oath nor does he have anyone to return to as and when he is released. In the absence of an oath, he is more free and less bound to any cause. The irony is that many detainees—Karanja, Gikonyo and several others confess their oath and ensure their release. His daring attempt to save Kihika's pregnant wife from being tortured becomes a living legend testifying to his humanity.

He walks to the dais like a hero and his daring admission of his betrayal of Kihika is both dramatic and anticlimactic. Following his confession, "Mugo felt light. A load of many years was lifted from his shoulders. He was free, sure, confident." (235) On seeing Lt. Konia and General R., he says: "I am ready" (for the trial). (238) This is heroic indeed for the one who "took refuge in reticence" (66) and lived like a hermit. Eileen Julien treats Mugo as the hero of the novel and identifies him with the reader. She observes: "Mugo—in his complexity, resembles the reader. He wants desparately to be integrated into the whole but is isolated by his crime and guilt." [21] Mugo's courageous confession puts most people to shame as they feel stripped naked from within. Ochola-Ojero comments: "Humanity's task is to face upto the problem of shared guilt, for to err is human." [22] Most people hang their heads in shame for Mugo and on their own behalf due to their own consciousness of their sense of betrayals, lapses and for all their misdeeds or indifference during a critical phase of their history. Thus, Mugo "is human in both the most glorious sense and in the most pathetic sense, such that his admission of his human nature is a victory—not for absolute virtue but for humanity." [23]

VI

Kihika is the underground leader of the Mau Mau rebellion during the Emergency. Unlike Gatu and Mugo, he enjoyed everything in life – the love of his parents, brother, sister, and at least two women (one of whom he marries) who are prepared to die for him (indeed they died for him – of course as part of the liberation struggle). He would always carry his Bible with him wherever he went. Besides the love and warmth of his kith and kin, he has his religious faith to sustain him in his moments of tension and adversity.

He kills Robson, the man-eater (Sr. District Officer). He explains to Mugo why he and all those fighting the war against colonialism resort to violence. He says: "We are not murderers. We are not hangmen – like Robson – killing men and women without cause or purpose." (190) Kihika is Ngugi's version of Fanon. Fanon also endorses counter-violence in the context of colonialism. It restores, according to Fanon, humanity to a fighting rebel. Jean-Paul Sartre in his Preface to Fanon's *The Wretched of the Earth* observes:

> When the peasant takes a gun in his hands, the old myths grow dim and the prohibitions are one by one forgotten. The rebel's weapon is the proof of his humanity. For in the first days of the revolt you must kill: to shoot down a European is to kill two birds with one stone, to destroy an oppressor and the man he oppresses at the same time: there remain a dead man, and a free man; the survivor, for the first time, feels a national soil under his foot.[24]

Robson's killing by Kihika needs to be interpreted on these lines. Kihika also emphasises the need for unity which is absolutely essential to fight against a deadly enemy. He says: "Because a people united in faith are stronger than the bomb." (191) Kihika sees himself as "the chosen instrument of god to deliver the Kikuyu from colonial bondage."[25] He uses the white man's religion of Christianity and his Bible to point out the gap between his word and deed; his promise and performance; and his speech and practice. The Kikuyu are aware of "the contradiction between the white man's teachings and his behaviour. They reject his actions but embrace his creed."[26] He also explains in the clearest possible terms how they were robbed of their lands:

> We went to their church. Mubia, in white robes, opened the Bible. He said: 'Let us kneel down to pray.' We knelt down. Mubia said: 'Let us shut our eyes.' We did. you know, his remained open so that he could read the word. When we opened our eyes, our land was

> gone and the sword of flames stood on guard. As for Mubia, he went on reading the word, beseeching us to lay our treasures in heaven where no moth would corrupt them. But he laid his on earth, our earth. (15)

This is how the white man 'cast a spell' of magic over them initially through the opium of his religion. When they woke up from this spell, the sword and later on the gun were aimed at them to bring about the pacification of the natives.

Kihika seeks shelter at Mugo's hut after he (Kihika) had killed Robson and tells Mugo about the same. He also asks Mugo to meet him at a secret place at an appointed time. Mugo, in turn, shares the secret with the white man betraying the confidence reposed in him by Kihika. Kihika is captured and hanged by the white administration.

VII

Like Captain Winterbottom of *Arrow of God*, John Thompson, the District Officer in *A Grain of Wheat* is also guided by and obsessed with his own moral vision of civilizing a dark continent. In the fashion of George Allen of *Things Fall Apart*, he (JT) also wanted to give a concrete shape to his mission in Africa by way of a book, "Prospero in Africa." The grand design of the book would enshrine in it the virtues of the English way of life based on "Reason, Order and Measure" (53); the benefits of British imperialism; the holy mission of administering an inferior race; (JT gloated over the idea with a thrill which he theorises: "to administer a people is to adminster a soul") (55); The French Colonial policy of Assimilation; Lord Lugard's Retrogade concept of Indirect Rule: Assessment of the native's character (According to him, the African is "a born actor . . . finds it easy to lie" [56]) in terms of an inferior status and his indulgence in senseless violence; and the interpretation of Mau Mau as a symbol of "anarchy" and "evil." In other words, *Prospero in Africa* "aims at the just ordering of human society" with "the creation of one British nation, embracing peoples of all colours and creeds, based on the just proposition that all men were created equal." (54) It is not difficult for anybody to see the basic contradiction here. *Prospero in Africa* is an anti-thesis to *The Wretched of the Earth*. Thompson chases this moral vision of the British Imperialism like a demon and in the process is distanced from his fellow colonial officers, the natives and even from his wife, Margery. He shares something in common with his opposite number, Kihika. This is his predicament in Africa despite his long innings in different capacities there since the

World War II. He is "at the centre of the drama in the colonial administration." (54)

Thompson was also "at the centre of the scandal at the Rira" (163) detention camp where eleven detainees were tortured to death. It rocked the British Parliament and shocked the conscience of the civilized world. On the eve of the Uhuru, Thompson is shaky, nervous and feels betrayed and has an image of himself as a "martyr." The egocentric Thompson realizes at last, with 'agony' and 'silent pain' that nobody is indispensable in a system and in the scheme of things. He wanted to check this with his wife. He had some curiosity to know if she would have turned to "another man had he died at the Rira Camp" the day before or some other time. Little does he realize that she did turn to "another man" while he was still alive and kicking.

As Thompson's "moral vision" of civilizing the Africans is shattered on the eve of Uhuru, he had resigned and made preparation to return home. He was "pinched by sadness at the knowledge that the Duke would sit to see the flag lowered, never to rise again on this side of Albion's shore." (41) It was all the more accentuated as he relived the incident of the 1952 when the Queen (a very young Princess then) shook hands with him. The thrill of that experience clung to his memory. Thompson found himself busy even on his last day in office in colonial service, sorting out papers, peering through important files and making notes.

A farewell party of the whites was arranged at Githima hostel on the eve of the departure of the Thompsons from Githima and Africa. Mrs. Dickinson, the librarian, fearing 'a holocaust' after Uhuru, made arrangements to flee to Uganda along with her boy friend, Roger Manson. Dr. Lynd feels insecure but she does not want to leave Githima as she cannot bring herself to the loss of her property. Everybody gets drunk as the party goes on late into the night. Thompson's glass slips off his hand and crashes on the floor causing anxiety to everybody around. The image of Thompson's "empty hand . . . in the air as if holding a glass to his mouth" (166) evokes a feeling of an eerie uneasiness, and a sense of irreconcilable loss.

On their way back, Thompson stops the car at the very spot where Dr. Van made love to Mrs. Thompson as though "to accuse" and mock her. He lights two cigarettes and smokes furiously, he says: "this is not the journey's end. . . . We are not yet beaten. Africa cannot, cannot do without Europe." (166) What follows then is the transformation of colonialism into "neo-colonialism"—only change of actors at the centre stage, black Zombies in place of white masters. But the flute player and the tune-caller remain the same. *A Grain of Wheat* fictionalises the drama of colonial rule, Uhuru and betrayals at several stages preceding independence.

VIII

A Grain of Wheat was written at Leeds where Ngugi was a student and the prevalent radical atmosphere at the University of Leeds was 'systematizing' his thinking in relation to the issues of poverty, growing inequalities the world over and the increasing friction between Capitalism and Communism. His research supervisor, Arnold Kettle, who himself was a Marxist also influenced Ngugi's thinking considerably. It was a few weeks before he started writing *A Grain of Wheat*, Ngugi stumbled on Fanon's *The Wretched of the Earth*. Fanon's scientific analysis of colonialism in psychological terms and the theory of violence with an additional dimension of 'racism' in a colonial context, is yet another strong influence on Ngugi.

The original title of the novel was conceived as "Wrestling with God." The novel has a religious dimension to it with scope for "the will of God," "destiny" and 'fate'—the kind of jargon which is antithetical to a Socialist/Marxist ideology. *Petals of Blood* is also concerned with the issues of religion and rebellion not as antithetical, but as a complement to each other. The chapter on *Petals of Blood* which follows this, explores this aspect in much greater depth. Ngugi is sought to be faulted by Peter Nazareth that Kihika does not use "Socialism" in his revolutionary utterance. [27] But as Shakespeare would say: 'What is in a name?' What really matters is not so much the language, the jargon as the "point of view" of the novel, the social philosophy of the novelist, the world-view in terms of the society and the kind of order it seeks to create. The novel seeks to underline that there cannot be much of a dichotomy between the essence of a true religion in its profundity and truth and Socialism (or Marxism in its ultimate analysis). The extremists of these faiths in their anxiety to deify what they believe in as the sole truth to the exclusion of all other finer values walk into the trap of fundamentalism unwittingly. The world needs to be guarded against fundamentalism of the narrow-minded practitioners of religion and the theoreticians of socialism for whom the theory as an abstraction is more fascinating than its essence and vitality in practice in the work-a-day world.

A Grain of Wheat is concerned with the egalitarian values of a people who seem determined to learn and cultivate the habit of living in harmony with each other in a spirit of mutual trust, respect and tolerance for one another. The novel urges the reader to examine his own inner self so as to discover his limitations and weaknesses, with a view to correcting the same in the larger interests of the community. Ngugi's "commitment" in the novel, his quest for a "just society" and egalitarian values – "remains the same throughout his career." [28]

Interestingly, his tools are religion and rebellion. *A Grain of Wheat* is also a "committed novel" as it "looks into the future because of its implied faith in the ability of a people to change their society." [29] *A Grain of Wheat* stresses the importance of struggle and sacrifice in the cause of freedom just as the grain of wheat as a seedling has to shed its identity and destroy itself in order to sprout into a sapling. Freedom of a nation blossoms out of the suffering and martyrdom of patriots to regenerate the nation and, as it were, die into life. It is also a transitional novel marking the novelist's progressive movement towards a socialist order as envisaged in his *Petals of Blood*.

The religious dimension of the novel is oriented to the socialist principle. There is an element of what we now call liberation theology in the utterances of Kihika who refuses to take a narrow, dogmatic view of organised Christianity. The effort and the struggle are paramount for achieving justice and egalitarianism – which far from contradicting the Christian position as the *synequanon* of religion and godly dispensation. Religion which is ordinarily associated with no-changers who uphold the status quo should be radically interpreted to signify change, reformation even rebellion to realize humanistic values and socialistic goals.

IX

The novel ends on a note of reconciliation and optimism. Mugo's confession compels Gikonyo to indulge in self-introspection. Besides, Gikonyo's mother is unhappy with his behaviour towards Mumbi. She tries to convince him how he has "broken his home" by refusing to realize what had "happened" during his absence from home. She says: "Read your own heart, and know yourself." (177) The image of the "broken home" makes him realize the need to set it right, or probably build a new one, and above all, the need to read one's own heart in order to know oneself – is also the message and an important motif in the novel. The novel seems to suggest that "one's goal in life should be to live heroically, to seek the truth about oneself, to face one's choices honestly, and to bear responsibility for one's deeds." [30]

Prompted by Mugo's confession, and his mother's wise counsel, Gikonyo invites his wife, Mumbi, to join him again and implores her to return "to the house, light the fire, and see things don't decay." (247) Mumbi is mellowed but a little hesitant in accepting the proposal, allows a little time for the message of Gikonyo to sink in her fully. She says:

> No, Gikonyo. People try to rub out things, but they cannot. Things are not so easy. What has passed between us is too much to be passed over in a sentence. We need to talk, to open our hearts to one another, examine them, and then together plan the future we want. (247)

Herein lies a ray of hope. The readiness to come together "to talk" and sort out the problems as equals (both man and wife) is itself a positive pointer towards reconciliation.

The very idea of "planning together" as if to write a new chapter in man-woman relationship is itself significant. The stage is set for reunion between Mumbi and Gikonyo. On his part, Gikonyo, at last, gives a definite and concrete shape to the pattern he proposes to carve on the stool he has been contemplating for long—to present to Mumbi as his marriage gift.

The pattern would be "a woman big-big with child." (247) The novel, blissfully, closes on this image as though to break the sense of shame and the spell of gloom generated by Mugo's confession. The proposed fresh pattern on the stool as contemplated by the carpenter husband of Mumbi is both regenerative and creative. It symbolically heralds the birth of "a new Kenya" in the image of Mumbi as a pregnant woman both as the mother of the Kikuyus and as the wife of Gikonyo.

NOTES

1. Ngugi wa Thiong'o, *A Grain of Wheat* (London: William Heinemann, 1967, Reset and revised in African Writers Series, 1986).
2. Ngugi, "The Writer in a Changing Society," *Homecoming* (London: Heinemann Educational Books, 1972), p. 47.
3. *Ibid.*, p. 50.
4. *Ibid.*, p. xv.
5. Govind Narain Sharma, "Ngugi's Christian Vision: Theme and Pattern in *A Grain of Wheat*," *African Literature Today,* No. 10 (1979), p. 167.
6. Leslie Monkman, "Kenya and the New Jerusalem in *A Grain of Wheat*," *African Literature Today*, No. 7 (1975), p. 111.
7. Govind Narain Sharma, p. 170.
8. Peter Nazareth, "Is *A Grain of Wheat* a Socialist Novel?" *An African View of Literature*, p. 136.

9. *Ibid.*
10. Govind Narain Sharma, p. 173.
11. *Ibid.*
12. Peter Nazareth, p. 132.
13. Shatto Arthur Gakwandi, "Commitment," *The Novel and Contemporary Experience in Africa* (London: Heinemann, 1977), p. 109.
14. Peter Nazareth, p. 132.
15. Leslie Monkman, p. 112.
16. *Ibid.*
17. Gakwandi, p. 119.
18. C. B. Robson, *Ngugi wa Thiong'o*, p. 53.
19. Peter Nazareth, p. 130.
20. C. B. Robson, p. 58.
21. Julien Eileen, "Heroism in *A Grain of Wheat*," *African Literature Today* (1983), p. 142.
22. Ochola-Ojero, "Of Tares and Broken Handles," *Busara*, Vol. 3, No. 2 (1970), p. 43.
23. Julien Eileen, p. 142.
24. Jean-Paul Sartre, "Preface" to *The Wretched of the Earth* (England: Penguin, Rev. ed., 1980), p. 19.
25. Gakwandi, p. 113.
26. *Ibid.*
27. Peter Nazareth, p. 146.
28. Chimalum Nwankwo, "Sifiting the Grain from the Husk: An Overview of Ngugi's Writing," *The Literary Half-Yearly*, XXVI (January 1984), p. 2.
29. Gakwandi, p. 108.
30. Julien Eileen, p. 144.

Religion and Rebellion
Petals of Blood

> . . . had he not handled live bullets, ready to die, which was the ultimate measure of one's commitment to the cause of a people's liberation?[1]

Like *A Grain of Wheat*, *Petals of Blood* is also a committed novel. It adresess itself to the politics of revolution and a socialist programme. While *A Grain of Wheat* focuses its attention on the vital issues plaguing the nation at the time of independence of Kenya in 1963, *Petals of Blood* seeks to survey the unpleasant events of the neo-colonial scenario of the country between 1963 and 1975. In addition to a number of book reviews and a score or more of critical essays which the novel provoked immediately after its publication, the "two international conferences – one in France, the other in California – have had sessions devoted to explication and analysis of its artistic and ideological features." [2] A few titles of critical essays on *Petals of Blood* provide an insightful perspective as to the nature, content and quality of the novel in terms of its objectives and ideology. Some of the prominent titles are given below:

Class Struggle and the Socialist Vision [3]
Towards a New Socialist Order [4]
As a Mirror of the African Revolution [5]
A Novel of the People [6]
As a Popular Novel [7]
As a Political Novel [8]
Optimism in *Petals of Blood* [9]
The Second Home Coming: Multiple Ngugis in *Petals of Blood* [10]
Africa and the Heroic Whore: Female Images in *Petals of Blood* [11]

These very titles are indicative of the mood, meaning and message of the novel. The last cited essay offers an excellent and objective analysis of the female images in the novel.

According to Bernth Lindfors, *Petals of Blood* is "Africa's first proletarian popular novel."[12] Chidi Amuta looks at it as "a classic of epic proportions in the emergent tradition of anti-imperialist literature in Africa" and Ngugi is concerned in the novel with his "search for socialist alternatives."[13] Indeed, all such critical appraisals of the novel are apt and appropriate. But the novel is much more than this. It has yet another important dimension which needs to be explored in much greater depth than what has been attempted so far. What Ngugi does in this novel is to work out his strategy through a religious framework in spite of his mistrust and contempt for Christianity as an organised establishment. The approach of the novelist is synthetic and multi-dimensional. He seems to be of the view that at the ultimate level both religion and socialism meet and mix. In a vital sense, and in my considered view, the novel could be interpreted as a study in religion and rebellion.

The novelist's quest for a world, a new idealized world free from greed and competitive accumulation appears to be Utopian at one level and also attainable at another. The scope of the novel has provision for people's liberation struggles on the one hand and a sense of faith in 'fate,' "destiny," 'the will of God' and so on and so forth. The politics of neo-colonialism in the form of multi-nationals and the comprador bourgeoisie; the issues arising out of religion and rebellion, constitute an important matrix of the novel. The thematic principle of the novel also seeks to deal with the law of God, the law of the state, and the socialistic goals. *Petals of Blood* is also remarkable for its reiteration of protagonism. The well-evolved concept of protagonism as discernible in *A Grain of Wheat* finds its most mature manifestation in *Petals of Blood*. In this novel of multiple protagonists, there is not one single hero who could be termed complete or central—without the necessary and complementary roles of other protagonists. Ngugi invests the marginal people with streaks of heroism—thereby emphasising that the true saviours are liberators or are the people themselves in their collective wisdom and might. Alamin Mazrui and Lupenga Mphande's observations in this regard are worth mentioning:

> as Ngugi has become more and more of a political activist, he has down played the individual aspect of leadership in favour of collective leadership . . . one no longer gets the impression that the destiny of the movement is in the hands of individual leader, the hero, the redeemer. . . . By portraying "revolution" as a process of collective intellect and action, Ngugi has in fact vested in every individual an element of leadership.[4]

Abdulla, Munira, Karega and Wanja—the protagonists of the novel—

share a collective fate as exiles at Ilmorg, a tiny remote place unexposed to modern civilization initially. To look at any one of them as the central hero will be, in my opinion, a misreading of the novelist's sense of protagonism. For instance, Eustace Palmer, in his assessment of *Petals of Blood* considers Munira as the "hero of the novel."[15] C.B. Robson in his full-length study of *Ngugi wa Thiong'o* says: "The central figure of the novel is Munira."[16]

Yet another significant feature of the novel is that Ngugi's protagonists represent three generations of colonial, neo-colonial and the era of liberation struggles (as symbolised in Karega and Joseph of the later times). The novel also has a secular side to it with representation for the indigenous Gikuyu leadership; Abdulla, a Muslim and his orphan-brother named by him Joseph and Munira who hails from an orthodox Chrisitian background.

Despite a sense of terrible and gloomy atmosphere pervading the novel on account of the neo-colonial situation, it offers a ray of hope and optimism in the tradition of socialist realism. This is integral to Ngugi's commitment in the novel. This chapter attempts to study Ngugi's sense of commitment in terms of religion and rebellion with reference to the vital areas of human experiences and social relationships.

Any critical appraisal of *Petals of Blood* has necessarily to address itself to how the lives of all the protagonists are interlinked in a very complex and intriguing social relationship and to what extent they share and differ from one another in their perspectival framework and ideological outlook. Each protagonist is subtly connected with the history of the nation in its making and is also a living witness to the transformation of the tiny, remote and unknown rural Ilmorg into a modern and urbanized capitalist complex both as an accident of history and under the influence of capitalism. Little wonder then that both the history of Ilmorg and by extension, the history of Kenya and Africa at large, acquire the prominence of a protagonist in the novel. According to Simon Gikandi, "Ilmorg is the fifth character in Ngugi's novel." [17] The following pages demonstrate how Ngugi invests each of his character with a considerable measure of heroism and commitment and how a collectivist commitment emerges finally for the dawn of a New Kenya from the contextual situation of the novel.

II

It is significant to note that the first three parts of the novel (it has in all four parts) are cast and captioned in terms of Biblical allusions and the climactic act of arson is committed by none other than Munira. The captions of the first three parts are: *Walking; Toward Bethlehem;* and *To Be Born.* These captions convey not only the religious symbolism of the novel but also are expressive of the journey motif. "To Be Born" is striking at once as an adaptaion of the phrase from "Second Coming" of W.B. Yeats. It reminds one of its vast store-house of associations as symbolized in the "Second Coming" and the other allied symbols of the poem. The journey motif and "To Be Born" have a particular relevance in the context of the novel reminiscent of "The Long March" for a new kind of order. Besides, "To Be Born" is yoked on to the last part captioned *La Luta Continua*! (the struggle continues). This is how Ngugi builds bridges to join together the divergent streams of religion and rebellion. The novel also abounds in Biblical allusions.

The novel begins as a 'Whodunit,' "a detective mystery."[18] The very opening of the novel is arresting at once. At one level, it reads like a crime thriller with Munira about to be arrested. The two cops who come to arrest him are nervous and shaky as they find Munira's Bible open at "Revelations" and the latter talking about chaos and violence as envisioned in the Second Coming. Munira is unnerved at the sight of the cops, and keeps his cool and speaks with a sense of detachment. He says: "We must always be ready to plant the seed in these last days before His second coming All the signs—strife, killing, wars, blood are prophesied here." (2)

Of all the protagonists in the novel, Munira is the most complex and baffling. He hails from an orthodox and wealthy Christian family. He does not mince words as to how his father built his assets and fame by foul and corrupt means: "His father Ezekieli, tall, severe in his austere aloofness, was a wealthy landowner and a respected elder in the hierarchy of the Presbyterian Church. He was tall and mean in his austere holiness." (13) Besides, he was hand in glove with the colonial administration. Munira's attention is often drawn to a photograph of his father standing by a gramophone with the legendary dog "sitting on its hind legs barking out: HIS MASTER'S VOICE." (91) This image of his father tends to cause discomfiture to him. The ill-gotten wealth and dubious fame of his father; the orthodox behaviour of his wife (her "silent prayers before and after making love," in particular); the social status and prestigious position of all his brothers and sisters; the untimely and tragic death of his sister Mukami by suicide (she alone in the family had a soft corner for him); and the constant nagging of his father for his easy and amoral ways of living—produce a kind of revulsion in him for the family. He feels thoroughly alienated not only from his family but the mainstream of life itself. Besides, he is haunted by a feeling of "failure," "non-being," "an outsider," "a spectator of life." In precise terms, his deliberate and conscious attempt "not to choose" (a way of life) so as to be free from any serious involvements takes him to Ilmorg as an exile. The new surroundings of the place become a kind of sanctuary, and an "escape hole" (49) for him.

The greater part of the story of the novel is a written statement recorded by Munira of his reminiscences of the twelve years (1963-1975) since his arrival at Ilmorg. This was done at the instance of the Inspector Godfrey who is commissioned to probe into the triple murder case of the V.I.Ps. Yet another equally important factor responsible for the reconstruction of the plot by Munira is to emphasise the "operation of God's Law." [19] The case of arson fascinated him (the Inspector of Police) all the more because of the personalities (both victims and the accused) it brought together. Godfrey's description of these characters is noteworthy and also serves as an introduction to them. "Chui—an educationalist and business man; Hawkins Kimeria—a business tycoon; Mzigo—an educationist turned business man; Abdulla—a petty trader. Munira—a teacher and man of God Karega—a trade unionist; Wanja—a prostitute." The murder of the three persons (1-3) is reported as a national tragedy by the Press.

Of the four accused, Munira, the teacher-cum-man of God confounded the imagination of the Inspector and intrigued his incisive mind as to how a man of his background could bring himself to indulge in the kind of crime (arson) he had committed. He asked himself: "Could property, wealth, status, religion, plus education not hold a family together? What else could a man want?" (334) Unable to unravel this mystery behind Munira's action, he put it down to a kind of "religious fanaticism." (334) But he adds his own rider here according to which "such fanaticism was normally found among the poor." (334)

Indeed, the most intriguing issue of the novel is the motivation behind Munira's crime. What exactly are the factors which influenced Munira? Religious fanaticism as a reason for the crime explains away, rather than explain the complexities with which the problem is riddled. In fact, there seems to be a kind of ambivalence behind Munira's motivation for the crime.

Munira is largely influenced by his desire to save Karega from the evil influence of Wanja. His indulgence in arson needs to be carefully analysed. The act of arson was preceded by three major and significant incidents which happen in quick succession. He seems to have been immesely influenced by these incidents.

Firstly, Munira visits Wanja at her place along with Karega following the latter's return to Ilmorg after five years. Wanja seeks to describe the harsh realities of the neo-colonial situation and her sense of "ruthless logic" according to which in this world of ours "you eat somebody or you are eaten. You sit on somebody or somebody sits on you." (291) Karega feels stung by the needle sharp ruthless truth of her version of the neo-colonial world. He could not bring himself to accept this as the only reality and feels provoked to say: "Must we have this world? Is there only one world? then we must create another world, a new earth." (294) Karega reiterates the need for another world, "A new world."

Munira, the "man of God" (44) is baffled by the diametrically opposite worlds represented by Wanja and Karega. He leaves the place all of a sudden "as if driven by a demon." (294) Back home at his place that night, he begins to wonder as to the reality of 'another world,' 'a new world.'

Secondly, the ghastly murder of the lawyer (Karega's mentor) shocked the sensibility of the 'man of God.' He was terribly upset and did not go to Church that Sunday. He begins to realize that he has been 'a spectator of life' too long and that he ought to do something. Probably for the first time in his life, he finds himself 'on the verge of a decision.' (298)

Thirdly, on the same Sunday, he finds a procession of evangelists led by Lilian, formerly a call-girl whom he used to frequent. The transformed Lilian also "talked of a new earth, another world, that knew not classes and clans . . . the eternal law of God . . . a new earth and a new heaven." (298) These three incidents happen in quick succession. He is also haunted by his need to break the spell of being a 'spectator of life.' His quest for a connection prompts him to do something, to give him a sense of belonging. He prays to god: "Give me the strength, Lord, give me a steadfast will. . . . I had to take a drastic step that would restore me to my usurped history, my usurped inheritance that would reconnect me with my history." (227) And, at last, he finds a solution to his riddles and his prayer answered. Chidi Amuta offers a dialectical explanation for the act of arson by Munira when he says: "Munira sees the exploitation and decadence of society as manifestations of an evil world requiring divine purgation . . . when, therefore, he sets Wanja's brothel on fire, he sees himself as doing the will of God."[20] In his lengthy confessional, Munira mentions:

> And I truly beheld a new earth, now that Christ was my personal saviour, He would level mountains and valleys and would wrestle Satan to the ground and conquer the evil that is this world. New life with Christ in Christ. I accepted the law. My knees trembled. I humbled myself to the ground and cried: I accept, I accept. I felt tears of gratitude and joy. My years of agony and doubt and pursuit of earthly pleasures were over. (298-99)

Inspired by a divine feeling for justice; guided by a secular motivation; and actuated by a desire to save Karega from the "fatal embrace" of Wanja, Munira at last, chooses a definite course of action – which he had deliberately avoided all along. Munira takes the crucial decision to destroy evil by burning Wanja's "Sunshine Lodge" which fosters prostitution and the vicious agents of capitalism (Kimeria, Chui and Mzigo). Munira's rebellion, thus, manifests itself in his act of arson in the belief of burning down the corrupt social structure. He is of the view that Wanja's whorehouse "mocked God's work on earth." (333) He pours petrol on the doors of Wanja's Sunshine Lodge, sets it on fire, and walks quietly to the Ilmorg Hill from where he "watched the whorehouse burn, the tongues of flame from the four corners forming petals of blood, making a twilight of the dark sky." (333) With the burning of the whorehouse, he feels that he is "no longer an outsider, for he had finally affirmed his oneness with the Law." (333)

Interestingly enough, the act of arson by Munira is in fact a reenactment of the burning of a model of a house of a woman (one Amina) with whom he had an affair as an adolescent boy. Following this immoral act which began to weigh as a burden on his conscience, he "stole a match box, collected a bit of grass and dry cowdung . . . and burnt it. He watched the flames and he felt truly purified by fire. He went to bed at ease with himself and peaceful in his knowledge of being accepted by the Lord." (14) Finally, the grown-up and middle-aged Munira seeks to find his identity merging with the law of the universe through the same means – burning so as to have his quest for another world, a new earth and a new heaven realized.

III

Karega is already introduced as a trade-unionist. Unlike the detention of both Munira and Abdulla for the purpose of interrogation, Karega's arrest provokes workers of the trade union to storm the police station demanding his release. They had to be chased away and beaten up to restore nomalcy. The challenging mood of the workers is described in terms of those "walking to their strength" and "such a defiant confrontation with authority had never before happened in Ilmorg." (4)

Karega's initiation and his intimate alignment with trade-unionism actually takes place in the final phase of the novel. Earlier, in the fashion of the other protagonists, Munira, Abdulla and Wanja – he also arrives at Ilmorg as an exile carrying a "maimed soul" and seeking a cure to it. By the time he joins the fellow exiles, he is sufficiently hardened on account of three major incidents which seem to have shaped his attitude to the wealthy people of contemporary Kenya in particular and the neo-colonial situation in general. Expulsion from the Siriana school at a very early age; Mukami's suicide with whom he was passionately in love, and above all, his mother's plight as a farm-labourer at Munira's father's premises, affect his sensibility and psyche. Unable to find a meaningful occupation at "the university of the streets" (51) in independent Kenya, he arrives at Ilmorg "searching for a lost innocence, faith and hope." (46)

On his arrival at Ilmorg, he approaches Munira, introduces himself to the latter as the son of Miriamu and that he learnt about his brother's (Ndinguri, a play-mate of Munira and a Mau-Mau activist) death through Mukami and that he was a former student of Munira. All these revelations of Karega make Munira feel ill-at-ease as the latter wished to live at Ilmorg unknown and uninvolved in any matter of serious nature other than his school work.

To begin with, Karega is a *teetotaller* and refuses to share even beer with the other exiles. But the same Karega was found drunk and quarelling in a bar. Wanja and Munira rescue him from his "drunken stupor," (103) a pathetic situation which is sought to be described in poignant terms by Eustace Palmer: "because of his integrity and idealism Karega is persecuted by this society and forced to drift from menial job to menial job. There could be no more powerful symbol of the destruction of potential than Karega in a drunken stupor."[21] When he comes to his senses, he agrees to return to Ilmorg at the instance of Wanja as though it was 'a covenant with fate.' He accepts with gratitude the offer of a teacher's post by Munira at the latter's Primary School.

It happens to be a very bad season of drought for the rural Ilmorgians. Karega feels an urge to do something to alleviate the plight of the Ilmorgians hit by a severe drought. He regrets that he and Munira were indulging in 'a gigantic deception' like 'two ostriches burying their heads in the sand of a class room ignoring the howling winds and the sun outside.' (110) Unlike Munira's, "Karega's relationship with Ilmorg is active; he relates to the town and its people in such a way that they shape his vision and understanding of the neo-colonial situation; in the same vein, he influences and shapes the community's sense of itself and its ironic fate." [22]

Munira decides to close the school considering the drought as 'an act of God.' Karega joins issue with him and says: "Why should people accept any act sof God without resistance? God, it is said, helps those who help themselves." (112) These two statements represent the diametrically opposite points of view of Munira and Karega. While the former tends to accept everything as an act of God and that nothing can be done to alter it, the latter emphasises the role of human effort to change the order of things, which in turn will be endorsed and appreciated by God. In precise terms, while Munira believes in a kind of determinism, Karega affirms the dialectical principle and seeks to graft it on to the divine will. Karega's idea of connecting "God's will" to human effort marks him off from rabid fundamentalism distinguishing him as a liberal thinker who attempts to link up genuine religious sensibility with the socialistic principle.

At the instance of Karega, the villagers decide to go to Nairobi to represent their problems to their M.P. The pilgirmage 'Towards Bethlehem,' rather the Long March heading towards Nairobi begins. According to Simon Gikandi, the motif of "journey is central to the character's process of self-understanding. It appeals to Karega's idealism and accentuates his search "[23] "for the meaning of the riddle at the meeting-point of the ironies of history, appearance and reality, expectation and actual achievement." (127) The journey, thus, is used as a powerful symbol in the novel. Explaining the significance of the journey, Ngara observes:

> In *Petals of Blood*, the journey operates at two levels. On one level, this is the physical journey . . . on the other, the whole book is conceived as a journey. . . . The phrase Walking Toward Bethlehem To Be Born Again covers the entire book . . . as a journey toward Bethlehem for a rebirth. The closing slogan *La Luta Continua* . . . was used by some African liberation movements such as Frelimo of Mozambique and the Zimbabwe African National Union (ZANU) in their struggle for liberation.

The pilgrims arrive at Nairobi tired and battered. They are greeted by scorn and contempt everywhere. They realize to their dismay that they are unwanted by those representing religion, politics and business. The first place they knock at turns out to be the mansion of a religious man, Rev. Jerrod, who sends them away with "empty prayers." Karega could not stand the hypocrisy of the religious man, calls him a "holy bastard" who would offer them only "the food of the spirit, the bread and fish of Jesus." (149) The other places they try turn out to be much worse. As they step into the place of Kimeria, they are subjected to further humiliation – the latter trying to seduce Wanja once again.

Ultimately, they manage to meet their M.P. Nderi wa Riera, who has the audacity to advise them to sell their cattle and other live stock rather than allow them to die of starvation and warns them against the intervention of outsiders. The crowd becomes restive and the M.P. is hit on the nose by a stone. He is on the run to the nearest police station. Munira, Karega and Abdulla are detained for a night. Their detention is reported in the press with a sensational caption:

DEATH IN DESERT: HUNGER IN ILMORG
DONKEY ON A RESCUE MISSION

A Nairobi-based-lawyer known for his socialist ideology secures their release, takes them to his place, treats them warmly and shares with them his own understanding of the neo-colonial situation of which he is a part. Obviously, the mission of the pilgrims fails, but in the process, they are transformed and born anew with a new awareness about their situation, the prevalent social inequalities and the reasons for the same. They return to Ilmorg sadder but wiser.

Back home, Karega writes to the lawyer requesting him to send some books. The lawyer sends him books on political science, history and imaginative literature written by university professors. Karega is appalled to find these learned professors "delighted in abusing and denigrating the efforts of the people and their struggles in the past." (199) He could not stand the distortion of truth related to the struggles of resistance to both colonialism and neo-colonialism as discernible in "the academic zombiesm and intellectual flankeyism" [25] of the learned scholars. Further, the same critic adds: "The novel pinpoints the buffoonery, inanity, obscurantism and apologia for imperialism which characterize the scholarship of African professors and so called educators trained in imperialist universities and other institutions of higher learning." [26] Disappointed, Karega packs the books and sends them back to the lawyer. The lawyer answers the queries raised by Karega and writes back: "You serve the people who struggle; or you serve those who rob the people . . . choose your side." (200) The lawyer's advice asking him to "choose" his "side" in a situation of the "robbers" and the "robbed," appeals to Karega's "infinitely analytical mind" providing him with "an ideological clarity," [26] he has been looking for.

A significant event of this phase is the toxic influence of the *Thenge'ta drink* brewed by Nyakinyua, Wanja's grand mother, on all the protagonists who find themselves narrating their personal lives in a confessional mode. Karega's mention of Ndinguri as his elder brother revives the memory of Abdulla of the Mau-Mau rebellion in which they were involved together. Karega reclaims his dead brother with a sense of pride: "had he [Ndinguri] not handled live bullets, ready to die, which was the ultimate measure of one's commitment to the cause of people's liberation?" (228) Karega also refers to his affair with Mukami and her subsequent suicide adding to the discomfiture of Munira. He happens to mention the names of Mukami and Wanja together accentuating the wounded feelings of Munira.

Munira takes exception to Karega's linking the name of his beloved sister Mukami with Wanja (whom he calls a VIP, a Very Important Prostitute). Karega joins issue with him and remarks in an emotional outburst:

> We are all prostitutes, for in a world of grab and take, in a world built on a structure of inequality and injustice, in a world where some can eat while others can only toil, some can send their children to schools and others cannot, in a world where a prince, a monarch, a businessman can sit on billions while people stare or hit their heads against church walls for divine deliverance from hunger, yes, in a world where a man who has never set foot on this land can sit in a New York or London office and determine what I shall eat, read, think, do only because he sits on a heap of billions taken from the world's poor, in such a world, we are all prostituted . . . why then need a victim hurl insults at another Victim? (240)

The emotional outburst of Karega seeks to strip naked the unpalatable harsh realities arising out of the neo-colonial situation which not only prostitutes most people but makes them all victims. Subsequently, Munira and Karega fall out. Karega leaves Ilmorg following his dismissal from the school engineered by Munira.

With the departure of Karega from Ilmorg, the novel enters its final phase of struggle (*La Luta Continua*). Karega becomes a hawker, sells fruits and sheep-skins for a while and undertakes many odd jobs before his initiation and active participation in the trade-union movement. He is committed to work for "a world in which the wealth of our land shall belong to us all, in which there will not be parasites dictating our lives, in which we shall all be workers for one another's happiness and well-being." (327)

When one takes a critical look at some of these statements of Karega, one wonders whether it is the novelist's surrogate representing his own ideology. Many a critic of *Petals of Blood* assailed Ngugi that the novel is more a polemic and a piece of propaganda than a work of art and fiction. For instance, Robson observes: "Conveying information is a legitimate part of a novelist's role, but in *Petals of Blood* Ngugi goes beyond what is acceptable in fiction, he is giving us polemic."[27] Most of the critics who find it difficult to accept and swallow the message and the mode of its delivery by Ngugi through *Petals of Blood* resort to criticism of this kind which Achebe calls "Colonialist Criticism."

Petals of Blood kicks up the controversy about the borderline separating art and ideology or propaganda versus imaginative fiction. But the question is whether art and ideology are two separate and distinct entities or are they two sides of the same coin? Lewis Nkosi's comment is apt and pertinent on the art-ideology nexus. He says: "Neither is art reducible to ideology, although it enjoys a close existence with ideology." [28] Further, Nkosi quotes Terry Eagleton so as to substantiate how art and ideology very often tend to meet and mix in the same matrix. Indeed, "art is so ideologically powerful . . . precisely because it is not just propaganda." [29]

Chidi Amuta's *The Theory of African Literature* seeks to settle the art - ideology controversy in a new light when he observes: "Against the timid imputations of bourgeoisie critics the decisive ideological thrust of *Petals of Blood* does not weaken its artistic identity. On the contrary, the strength of the novel derives precisely from the sheer aesthetic force of its informing and objectified ideology." [30] Quoting Lenin, Kamenju comments: "Lenin singled out as one of the characteristic features of the epoch we are living in the struggle for national liberation of the oppressed nations against the imperialism of the oppressor nations." [31] The problems plaguing the so-called independent states of the present century are due to the oppression of imperialism and the solution to it cannot be in any manner other than socialist terms attainable through perseverant struggles.

In any case, Karega is back in Ilmorg after five years. He visits all his former friends and finds Ilmorg transformed into a capitalist complex reducing Abdulla to a hawker once again and Wanja thrown into a world of whoredom with vengeance. He rejects the love and friendship of Wanja once for all as he feels she has thrown her lot with those of Kimerias and the like. Jennifer Evans interprets the behaviour of Karega towards Wanja in terms of his "critical attitude," moral righteousness and as "a virtue."

Karega, a more enlightened political visionary, likes to destroy the evil system by leading a workers' revolution. Karega, the active trade-unionist, returns home after a late night meeting, is arrested for being "a communist at heart" and condemned to confinement. He becomes weak in body due to torture and shocks to which he is subjected. And yet his belief in the ability of people to sustain the spirit of struggle remains unshaken. Thus, while Munira represents the religious view, Karega stands for socialist ideology. Both of them together seem to unify religion and rebellion for the realization of the ideal world in their respective individual terms.

IV

On the following morning of the death of Chui, Mzigo and Kimeria at Wanja's place in the arson from which he rescues Wanja, Abdulla was taken to the police station, where he was locked up in a cell and slapped.

He feels humiliated and enraged. He is referred to as "a petty trader" by the Inspector Godfrey. Abdulla is also an exile at Ilmorg like others.

On being asked by Karega as to why and what brought him to Ilmorg, Abdulla narrates the account of his involvement in the Mau-Mau along with Ndinguri. While Ndinguri was trapped carrying bullets to the underground activists and hanged a week later, Abdulla loses one of his legs in a shoot-out. He is incarcerated and released from detention on the eve of Uhuru (independence).

Abdulla is stunned and shocked at the insensitivity of the state to one like him, a former Mau-Mau, in independent Kenya. He could not stand being humiliated and heckled as he tries to rehabilitate himself as a one-legged-man. "The unsung hero" (243) of the freedom struggle, carrying the memory of it in his stump of a leg, prefers to remain "dumb" and "deaf" and go "deep-deep into the country where [he] would have no reminder of so bitter a betrayal." (255) Like his fellow exiles, he also arrives at Ilmorg along with his donkey to which he refers as his 'other leg' often. While the other exiles are "maimed" in their souls, Abdulla is maimed physically as well. Referring to Abdulla's crippled condition, Chidi Amuta observes: "Abdulla's amputated limb is a physical testimony to the sacrifices which the peasants had to make in the struggle for independence." [32] To begin with, he uses his donkey for transporting goods in the market of Ilmorg. Later on he establishes a small shop and a bar which registers instant success following Wanja's association with it as his bar-maid-cum-partner.

Abdulla prefers to hobble along with the marchers to Nairobi instead of taking a ride in his donkey-cart. He humours and entertains the Ilmorgians with his endless narration of tales all along the way. He becomes 'the hero of the journey' (134) and the compliment paid to him by Karega speaks volumes about Abdulla's courage, integrity and commitment. According to Karega, Abdulla represents "the best self of the community, symbol of Kenya's truest courage." (228)

Appreciating Abdulla's sense of humane qualities and generosity, Wanja says, "Abdulla, you have a big heart." (77) He shows his readiness to help others in trouble. He tries his best to prevail on Wanja to ensure her stay at Ilmorg when the latter is all set to leave the place in disgust. He offers her partnership in his business. Later, he sells all his assets to help her when she needed a lot of money to redeem the lands of her grandmother from being auctioned by a commercial bank. In the process, he allows himself to "return to the herd of victims" and becomes a hawker selling fruits and sheep-skins.

When Karega wanted to leave Ilmorg following his dismissal from school, Abdulla offers him full partnership in his business wanting to retain him there. He wanted Karega to marry Wanja as they were seen moving together like love birds. He says: "I ask you not to go away. For where will you go to? Stay a muhoi here. Get a strip of land. Grow a crop, like Wanja here. Perchance one or two will germinate and bear a fruit or two!" (256)

Abdulla springs a surprise on his fellow exiles by revealing the identity, rather the absence of identity of Joseph whom he picked up from a street while the latter was struggling hard to collect the left-over of food from garbage. He says: "I caught him [the orphan boy] . . . 'What is your name?' . . . I took him home." (286) That Joseph is not his brother is a big surprise to everybody. Karega is impressed a lot by the humanity of Abdulla and remarks: "If Abdulla could choose a brother, why couldn't they all do the same? Choose brothers and sisters in sweat, in toil, in struggle." (303) Abdulla not only chooses a brother but he takes every possible interest in the education of the boy on whom he pins his future hopes.

A plane surveying the trans-Africa road through Ilmorg crashlands killing Abdulla's donkey. He feels for the loss of his donkey as though he lost an intimate friend. The donkey is one of the most effective symbols used by Ngugi in *Petals of Blood*. Robson's comment that 'the donkey, almost reduces this ex-Mau-Mau fighter to an absurd level,' [33] seems to mistake the very mission for which it is intended. Palmer's interpretation of the donkey in terms of its association with its master and as 'a symbol' used by the novelist is convincing and rational. Palmer observes: "When the people, in a desperate bid, to propitiate the gods and end the drought, plan to use the donkey as a sacrificial victim and maim it, Abdulla correctly sees it as maiming of his other leg. The donkey has always been a symbol of sacrifice, the scapegoat that takes the beatings on behalf of society." [34]

Presence of the donkey in the novel as a source of great help and use to Abdulla is a sad commentary on the insensitivity of the post-independence Kenyan society towards its freedom fighters. The donkey as such "is one of the most effective symbols . . . by means of which the novelist tries to level his accusing finger at the contemporary Kenyan society for all its lapses, its cruelty and inhumanity towards the heroes of the freedom movement." [35]

Abdulla's sense of self-respect is tremendous. Wanja finds him dressed in rags and offers him money to buy clothes. He tears off the first bill from a wad of currency offered by her thinking that he would be "a dog to dress with money probably given her by Kimeria." (313) However, he is not unaware of the fact that it was she who was paying the school fees for Joseph.

He visits Wanja to share the happy piece of news with her regarding

Joseph's top ranks at school and in order to atone for his earlier behaviour. They are together for long talking late into the night. The late night meeting culminates in an unexpected and fruitful physical union between them. The invisible fate unites the lives of the resourceful Wanja with the cripple Abdulla. Consequently, they find a magic cure to their maimed souls.

Earlier, Abdulla also offers to marry Wanja as though to redeem her from the world of whoredom into which she had sunk. Abdulla, a Mau-Mau activist and cripple, is gracious and generous to his fellow exiles, Karega and Wanja, and by fostering an orphan boy with a lot of affection. By marrying Wanja, a public woman, he rises to sublime heights and plays an important role in the thematic structure of the novel. Her prostitution of herself makes him feel "personally humiliated by what seemed her irrevocable and final entry into whoredom. It hurt him . . . but he went on. 'Listen. Please. Stop this business. I have a little money. . . . Marry me. I may not be much to look at: but it was fate.'" (311)

Later on, he is admitted into her life as her partner. As he is invited to her "Sunshine Lodge" on the crucial night of arson, Abdulla vows to kill Kimeria himself and he evolves his own *modus operandi* for the same. By killing Kimeria, he hopes to avenge the death of Ndinguri and redeem Wanja from his clutches. Besides, by this proposed act, he also hopes to "regain the right to call himself a man." (316) But, once again the invisible law of fate or the element of utter unpredictability which governs human lives and events—intervenes as though to spare him the trouble of murdering Kimeria himself.

Abdulla languishes in his cell, takes the beatings and torture like a funeral ram and yet he displays rare signs of fulfilment probably due to his choice of Joseph who grows into a tall youth and for rescuing Wanja from the flames. He is also determined and committed to save Karega from the latter's involvement in the crime of arson. He carefully answers the queries of the interrogating officials keeping the safety of Karega in view. Thus, the delineation of Abdulla's character serves as a historical cover and connection in the novel besides being a symbol of struggle and sacrifice.

V

Wanja, one of the four accused, is sought to be interrogated for her alleged involvement in the crime of arson. But she continues to be 'in a delirium,' screaming "fire . . . fire" till the tenth day of her confinement in hospital. The image of fire is an obsession with her and she is haunted by it throughout. When she is finally cleared for interrogation on the twelfth day, she tries to narrate how she is tormented by the image of fire. She says: "fire is a nightmare in our family. My aunt died of arson. I left Bolibo Bar because a room I rented there was burnt." (321) Her final involvement for the third time in fire and flames accentuates her sense of fear and nervousness.

Wanja is invested with a fiercely feminine and aggressively individualistic personality. 'She belongs to that remarkable breed of Ngugi women – Mwihaki, Nyambura, Muthoni, Mumbi, Wambuku – all of them brave, resilient, resourceful and determined', says Eustace Palmer. According to Chidi Amuta, "Wanja is a typical Ngugi woman, elan vital combining great adaptive skills with dynamism, enterprise and forbearance." [37] Commenting on the role and place of women in Ngugi's fiction, Jennifer Evans observes: "In Ngugi's novels women are shown to have a fundamental role in the struggle against oppression and exploitation, and often courage and hope are ultimately found in their hands." [38] Wanja, thus, belongs to 'the strong breed of Ngugi women' in the throes of a social change.

Every African name has a meaning. Wanja implies an outsider. She arrives at Ilmorg as an exile nursing a wound in her soul caused by her own act of killing her child, (Kimeria's) unable to face the hostile world as an unwed-girl mother. The malady with which all the other exiles are afflicted is summed up by Wanja in poignant terms when she says, "We all carry maimed souls and we are all looking for a cure."(73) She desperately tries to atone this by conceiving again and by helping children in distress. She endures the punishment of remaining barren almost till the end of the novel. "Her barrenness," observes Jennifer Evans, "is not simply physical, but expressive of a deeper spiritual and emotional lack of fulfilment." [39]

Following the departure of Karega from Ilmorg, she is determined not to 'return to the herd of victims,' (294) like Abdulla. She becomes hardened, vindictive and allows herself to be guided by vengeance. She takes to big-time prostitution as though to seek her "burial in property and degradation" mistaking the same for a 'glorious achievement.' (328) Her brothel, "Sunshine Lodge" acquires the prominence of Rev. Jerrod's "All Saints Church."

Following Karega's return after five years, she implores him to stay with her for the night as he used to in the past. She says: "I have been so lonely. . . so lonely. This wealth feels so heavy on my head." (327) Karega feels touched but remains unmoved. He tells her bluntly that he and she can no longer be involved in any meaningful association as she has chosen to throw her lot with Kimeria and the like. He leaves the place abruptly as though driven out by a demon leaving her dazed and shocked. At this point of time precisely, Abdulla steps into her life as though to fill the vacuum created by the exit of Karega from her life. She allows him to make love to her and accepts him as her partner. Under these circumstances, it is very natural that she has chosen, at last, to share her lot and fate with Abdulla, the "man of big heart." However, Robson seems to have a different view of their (Abdulla-Wanja) final alliance when he says: "The final alliance with Wanja decreases rather than increases our acceptance of Abdulla." [40]

Wanja's final choice of Abdulla is a fitting finale and is in tune with her character and temperament. In fact, she "did not see any contradiction in her choice of Abdulla as her instrument of vengeance. It seemed only natural now that she had accepted him into her life," (328) a fact which Robson seems to miss or ignore.

Although Karega parted from her life for obvious reasons, he leaves behind the stamp of his personality and an indelible impression on her with regard to the "choice" one has to make in one's life without leaving scope for neutrality of any kind in a situation of "the robbers and the robbed."

Wanja carefully and meticulously plans out her vengeance on Kimeria by whom she was seduced when she was no more than an adolescent girl. she invites Abdulla also to her 'Sunshine Lodge' in addition to Mzigo, Chui and Kimeria. With the evidence of her murder of Kimeria destroyed, she would never tell anybody and much less the Inspector how she "had killed Kimeria . . . struck him dead with the panga she had been holding." (330)

Thus, Wanja not only chooses a partner, but also a new way of life trying to shed the skin of her prostituted body. Jennifer Evans' comment regarding Wanja's act of violence in Fanonist terms is worth mentioning: "Wanja's act of violence in this instance is an act of personal liberation, a kind of cleansing and revitalizing Fanonist violence." [41] Wanja, the outsider as her name implies, remains no longer so with the execution of her choices.

Besides, Wanja begins to feel the stirrings of life taking shape in her womb. Her pregnancy at this stage is a crowning glory, a grand finale besides being a fulfilment of her womanhood. Pressed closely by her mother as to whose child she was carrying, she depicts it not in oral terms, but by means of a pictorial representation on a wooden board with a piece of charcoal. The figure turns out to be a man: "Kimathi in his moments of triumph and laughter and sorrow and terror – but without one limb." (338) She gives the picture to her mother and feels a tremendous calm, contentment and pride. She, at last, finds a "cure" to her "maimed soul." Wanja sheds several of her images – an outsider, "a virgin whore," an "important prostitute" so that she acquires the image of a mother, purified and reborn as she is by the flames of fire. The image of fire in which the victims are reduced to ashes also implies a possible dismantling of the existing power structures with new ones on a new foundation.

Wanja, despised as a fallen woman, is a veritable source of solace and strength to the other characters at crucial stages. She gathers all strength and valour to murder the wicked tycoon, Kimeria. By marrying Abdulla, the cripple, she buries her past displaying rare nobility and courage. She is proud to be the mother of Abdulla's child—the representative of the new progeny of a brave new world.

VI

Petals of Blood ends on a note of optimism which is rekindled and reinforced by Karega's renewal of faith in a new kind of Kenya to be born out of struggles to be launched by the peasants and workers all over the country. In all probability, Joseph is likely to lead these struggles in his absence. Both of them are committed to a humane and socialist order of a promising "tomorrow."

Petals of Blood depicts the flowering (petals) of a new egalitarian and just order brought about by struggle and sacrifice (blood). Two major motifs stand out in ushering the new world; religion and rebellion. The titles of the three parts: "Walking," "Towards Bethelhem" and "To Be Born" have religious symbolism. The pilgrimage brings about an awakening and change in the protagonists to fight the effete and corrupt order for the establishment of a new civilization—which needs to be preserved and sustained through continuous vigilance and struggle by the community. This is well defined by the caption of the fourth part—*La Luta Continua* (The struggle continues).

The renewal of a promising and prosperous "tomorrow" as conveyed to him in his prison cell by a girl, Karega's hopes are rekindled. He imagines the dawn of a new world: "the kingdom of man and woman . . . enjoying and loving in creative labour." (344) This 'creative labour' is the prerequisite for the dawn of a new order.

NOTES

1. Ngugi wa Thiong'o, *Petals of Blood* (London: Heinemann, 1977).
2. Bernth Lindfors, "*Petals of Blood* as a Popular Novel," *Contemporary*

Literature, ed. Stepehn H. Arnold (Washington: Three Continents Press, 1983), p. 49.

3. Chidi Amuta, *The Theory of African Literature* (London: Zed Books, 1989), pp. 143-53.
4. Emmanuel Ngara, *Art and Ideology in the African Novel* (London: Heinemann, 1985), pp. 75-85.
5. Kamenzu Grantu, *Marxism and African Literature*, ed. George M. Gubelberger (London: James Currey, 1985), pp. 131-35.
6. Balagun F. Odun, *Ba Shiru*, X, 2 (1981), pp. 49-55.
7. Bernth Lindfors, pp. 49-50.
8. Simon Gikandi, *Reading the African Novel* (London: James Currey, 1987), pp. 111-48.
9. Indra Sena Reddy, *Kakatiya Journal of English Studies*, VIII (1987-88), pp. 135-43.
10. Peter Nazareth and G. Gubelberger, ed., *Marxism and African Literature*, pp. 118-30.
11. Jennifer Evans, *Contemporary Literature*, ed. Hal Wyliee, et al (Washington: Three Continents Press, 1983), pp. 57-65.
12. Berth Lindfors, p. 49.
13. Chidi Amuta, p. 143.
14. Alamin Mazrui and Lupenga Mphande, "The Historical Imperative in African Activist Literature," *UFAHAMU*, XXII, 2 (Spring 1990), pp. 56-57.
15. Eustace Palmer, *The Growth of the African Novel* (London: Heinemann, 1979), p. 194.
16. C.B. Robson, *Ngugi wa Thiong'o*, p. 93.
17. Simon Gikandi, p. 143.
18. Peter Nazareth and G. Gubelberger, p. 118.
19. Simon Gikandi, p. 137.
20. Chidi Amuta, *The Theory of African Literature*, p. 150.
21. Eustace Palmer, *The Growth of African Novel*, p. 301.
22. Simon Gikandi, p. 138.
23. *Ibid.*, p. 143.
24. Emmanuel Ngara, *Art and Ideology in the African Novel*, p. 77.
25. Grant Kamenju, "*Petals of Blood* as a Mirror of the African Revolution," *Marxism and African Literature*, p. 132.
26. *Ibid.*, p. 131.
27. Chidi Amuta, *The Theory of African Literature*, p. 151.
28. C.B. Robson, p. 101.
29. Lewis Nkosi, *Home and Exile* (London: Longman, 1965), p. 163.
30. *Ibid*. pp. 163-164.
31. Chidi Amuta, *The Theory of African Literature*, p. 148.

32. Grant Kamenju, p. 130.
33. Chidi Amuta, p. 146.
34. C.B. Robson, p. 100.
35. Eustace Palmer, *The Growth of African Novel*, p. 300.
36. Indra Sena Reddy, p. 139.
37. Eustace Palmer, p. 297.
38. Chidi Amuta, p. 150.
39. Jennifer Evans, "Mother Africa and the Heroic Whore: Female Images in *Petals of Blood*," *Contemporary Literature*, p. 57.
40. *Ibid.*, p. 63.
41. C.B. Robson, p. 100.
42. Jennifer Evans, p. 63.

Amaechina
(Let the Path-Never-Close)
Anthills of the Savannah

> The sweeping, majestic visions of people rising victorious like a tidal wave against their oppressors and transforming their world with theories and slogans into a new heaven and a new earth of brotherhood, justice and freedom are at best grand illusions. The rising, conquering tide, yes; but the millennium afterwards, no! New oppressors will have been readying themselves secretly in the undertow long before the tidal wave got really going.[1] (99)

Beatrice asks her young friends: "What must a people do to appease an embittered history." (220) This query of the female protagonist seems to be crucial in the context of *Anthills of the Savannah*. A quick look at the fictional scenario of Achebe from his *Things Fall Apart* to *A Man of the People* will help us find the clue. A discerning reader could well find in *Anthills* useful suggestions by way of a positive response to the query.

Things Fall Apart, No Longer at Ease and *Arrow of God* deal with the rise and fall of their respective individual protagonists whose unhappy and sad end could be attributed to the machinations of colonialism. To that extent, they evoke the sympathy and pity of readers. In *A Man of the People*, Achebe's target of attack is no longer a George Allen, a Winterbottom or a Green, but the indigenous political leadership as represented by Nanga, the protagonist in *A Man of the People* and the like. The novelist is thoroughly disillusioned with the rule of law by the new black-zombies who have stepped into the shoes of their erstwhile colonial masters. Chief Nanga's "princely seven bathroom mansion with its seven gleaming, silent action water closets," in a country "where the majority of the peasants and workers live in shacks and can afford only pails of excrement,"[2] strikes both as a symbol of corruption and as an unhappy contrast to the sordid predicament of the people. *A Man of the People*, Achebe's first post-colonial novel, marks a significant transition from the world of "goat-skin bags," "drinking horns" and make-shift hut-dwellings of *Things Fall Apart*.

People in *A Man of the People* begin to realize that the practising politicians have taken a greater share of the 'national cake' than they need and deserve and that they have started reaping where they have not sown. The political leadership is also shrewd enough to sense the mood of the people in such a situation and organizes rigging of elections on an unprecedented scale. It becomes a free-for-all and the forces of violence unleashed by the leadership boomerang on itself ultimately, culminating in a "military take-over" which "seemed a cathartic and pragmatic necessity at the time. But the euphoric interim of the military rule proved more fatal."[3] Unlike the first three novels of Achebe, *A Man of the People* represents a tragedy of values and it is a kind of dirge on the civilian rule paving the way for a succession of coups and change of governments at regular intervals in Nigeria.

While *A Man of the People* is a satire on the deplorable political scenario of the country immediately after independence (in the 1960s), *Anthills of the Savannah* is an indictment of the rule by the army in the last quarter of the present century. The remedy turns out to be worse than the disease. What then are the alternatives? Are there any? Is the history of Kangan (the fictional locale of the novel and "a thinly disguised Nigeria") alienated and 'embittered.'

Achebe is concerned with these issues in his latest novel which appeared after a gap of over two decades whereas his first four novels appeared in a fairly quick pace of less than a decade, between 1958 and 1966. Beatrice, Achebe's female "surrogate novelist,"[4] is anxious to know how an "embittered history" of a people could be appeased. This chapter seeks to discuss the issues revolving around the 'embittered' and 'alienated' history of a country in terms of power-equations and power politics and the role of a writer in a third-world country. The novel represents 'a canonical voice inscribed in the anti-imperialist discourse of the Third-world writing, which is still struggling to rewrite itself in the process of decolonization.'[5]

II

The novel has a dramatic start with Samson, the dictator, in tantrums and chiding his Cabinet Ministers for lack of vigilance on their part about the security of the state. It "opens with the military ruler of the African state of Kangan disdainfully treating his civilian Cabinet like children."[6] Like *Petals of Blood, Anthills of the Savannah,* has multiple protagonists and the story of the novel is sought to be told by means of a multiple narratology. But Achebe's novel is basically different from *Petals of Blood* in the sense that in the former, it is difficult to pinpoint and say that such and such a character is a villain. The real villain in *Anthills* is Power itself. Ikem, who seems to represent Achebe's viewpoint in many respects, comments: "Those who would see no blot of villainy in the beloved oppressed nor grant the faintest glimmer of humanity to the hated oppressor are patriots and party-liners." (100)

Man is an intermix of both good and evil in unequal proportions. The novel seeks to indict the right reactionaries as well as the left adventurists. Achebe seems to strike a middle-path based on the Igbo-concept of duality in things, one thing balancing and correcting the other. He also focusses on the significance and inevitability of contradictions governing and influencing events, and people. He observes: "Contradictions if well understood and managed can spark off the fires of invention. Orthodoxy whether of the right or the left is the graveyard of creativity." (100) A human being is neither wholly good, nor wholly bad, but a blend of the two. The potentialities for good and ill – the contrary forces in man if well recognised and managed will instil creative energy for a suitable intermix in the making of a better individual and community. The habit of looking upon any person or institution in terms of unadulterated black or white has to be given up and the Hegelian dialectics of thesis and antithesis merging into a higher synthesis needs to be explored in a new key – not necessarily Hegelian or Marxian. Herein lies Achebe's philosophical projections into creativity with its essential ingredients contained not in uniformity of regimentation of ideas but the principle of 'contradictions.'

Sam, the military dictator, Christopher Oriko, Commissioner for Information, Ikem Osodi, editor of the *National Gazette* (an official state organ), and Beatrice Okoh, a careerist-bureaucrat, attached to the Ministry of Finance are the principal protagonists in the novel. All of them are "been to's" and are educated in England. They know each other inimately for a fairly long time. Chris avers with a sense of pride: "We are all connected. You cannot tell the story of any of us without implicating the others. Ikem may resent me but he probably resents Sam even more and Sam resents both of us most vehemently. We are too close together." (66) This statement by Chris who knows Sam for over twenty years, is expressive of the resentment against one another because of the power-nexus between them. Beatrice retorts to say: "all three of you, are incredibly conceited. The story of this country, as far as you are concerned, is the story of the three of you." (66) Beatrice seems to have a better insight into each one of them and how their estrangement from one another originates and develops due to lack of adequate communications between them.

It is chance, rather than choice which puts Sam at the helm of affairs as His Excellency when the civilian rulers 'landed unloved and unmourned on the rubbish heap' (12) (a fate which ironically awaits this regime also) and the young Sandhurst-trained Commander (Sam) was invited by the even younger coup-makers to become the Head of the State. (12) The fall of the civilian rule is described by Sam's sycophant Cabinet Minister, Prof. Okong, in terms of 'a historic fall from grace to grass.' (12) Chris recollects with a sense of pride how he was not only invited to join Sam's Cabinet, but he found himself advising "a whole Head of State" on the choice of half-a-dozen ministers accounting for over fifty percent of the Cabinet positions. It was he who recommended Prof. Okong's name by placing it at the top of the list. Ikem succeeds Chris as the editor of *The Gazette* following the latter's elevation to the Ministry.

The issue then is: How do such intimate friends fall out soon so that each begins to suspect the moves and motivations of one another leading to mutual resentment and suspicion? No single explanation, I should think, is capable of answering this satisfactorily. A number of factors come into play for the dissensions among the once intimate friends leading to their estrangement. There seem to be temperamental differences among them. The triumvirate is also referred to as "three green bottles" by Chris, the implication being that they are prone and vulnerable to fall to pieces like the bottles any time. Chris is of the view that Sam is a good mixer and Socialite. John Kent, alias Mad Medico (referred to as MM throughout the novel), an English character, is a common friend of all of them. He alone continues to enjoy the liberty to address His Excellency as Sam. Paying glowing tributes to Sam of the college days, M. M says: "he was such a nice fellow in those days. He had a wholesome kind of innocence about him. He was morally and intellectually intact—a kind of virgin." (59) This was the image Sam enjoyed as a student at college before his contact and association with Power.

Ikem is 'romantic,' 'sentimental,' a 'revolutionary,' and 'a passionate crusader.' But, unfortunately, he "had no solid contact with the ordinary people of Kangan." (39) This lack of contact with the ordinary people goes home to all the other protagonists including Beatrice, because of their alien education and the European values imbibed by them.

Chris was content to be a sort of half-way-house between the Socialite Sam and intellectual Ikem. His 'career' typifies the avoidance of extremes.'[7] He says to Beatrice: "I have always been in the middle. Neither as bright as Ikem and not such a social success as Sam." (66)

In addition, he quotes from a children's song to say "the one in the middle is the child of luck." (66) Chris takes in his stride with a kind of passivity the unhappy, 'frigid' conjugal relationship with his American wife whom he married in London and separated from her after six months.

His two-year association with Sam and the Cabinet colleagues aggravates further his sense of passivity and develops in him a 'detached clinical interest' (2) towards matters of the state. In spite of this detachment, he gets in to the grooves of bossism which is part of power-game. He maintains: "Sam is now my boss and I am Ikem's boss." (65) Ikem, on his part, ridicules the concept of power-hierarchy and bossism in terms of 'circus' when he says: "Following a leader who follows his leader would be quite a circus." (54)

Power-game in the novel becomes synonymous with circus. Just as the wild animals are tamed into submission in a circus-show, people involved in power-game are sought to be rendered ineffectual and impotent by power-equations all along the line. That is why Sam's Cabinet is likened to "people you put away in a wooden locker" (57) where in people are equated with things without a voice or a soul of their own. The worst part of it is that the people themselves are also sought to be domesticated so as to render them pliable and docile. While the colonial rulers applied the theory of 'Pacification' (as in *Things Fall Apart*) to subdue the natives, the native rulers resorted to 'Domestication' (40) of their own subjects.

A major weakness with Sam is his sense of insecurity. Chris wonders why the army leader armed to the teeth should feel nervous and jittery at the sight of even a small group of people who keep visiting the big boss for favours of many kinds. It is only natural since the boss holds both "the yam and the knife."

Anthills of the Savannah is cast against the background of a delegation comprising six elders from Abazon who land at the Presidential Palace unannounced wanting to invite Sam to their province to atone for their opposition to him when he sought to install himself as the 'President-for Life' through a Referendum. They are also prompted by a compelling need to seek redressal for the drought which hit them hard. Incidentally, of the four provinces, Abazon alone voted against Sam in the Referendum for the Life Presidencey. Prof. Okong's account of the outcome of the Referendum is the very acme of grovelling sycophancy. He says: "Let us not flaunt the wishes of the people. . . . Your Excellency, three provinces out of four is a majority anywhere. . . . The people have spoken. Their desire is manifest. You are condemned to serve them for life." (5)

All this drama is enacted at the beginning of the novel. Achebe, thus, exposes the farthest limits of sycophancy and hypocrisy of those who surround the boss in any system or institution. Academic institutions and bodies are no exception. They keep parroting: Boss is always right. He can never be wrong. Such bunch of time-servers pose a potential threat to the very image of the boss (the boss seldom has a good image anyway) and his administration. The worst part of it is the boss is never allowed to have access to the truth which always gets distorted and biased to suit the immediate and long-range needs of the boot-lickers.

Prof. Okong belongs to the breed of boot-lickers and praises H. E. sky-high, equates him with Jesus by calling him the "Nation's Man of Destiny." (23) He and his band of colleagues in the Cabinet 'have no problem in worshipping' (24) the Man of Destiny. But Chris and Ikem can neither stand hypocrisy of this kind nor can they bring themselves to indulge in boot-licking. Ikem feels strongly about the antics of Sam's Cabinet and says: "Worshipping a dictator is such a pain in the ass."

Ikem tries relentlessly to prevail on Chris to save Sam from the clutches of the boot-licking "court-jesters." He observes :

> I am sure that Sam can still be saved if we put our minds to it. His problem is that with so many petty interests salaaming around him all day, like that shyster of an Attorney-General, he has no chance of knowing what is right. And that's what Chris and I ought to be doing—letting him glimpse a little light now and again through chinks in his solid wall of court jesters; we who have known him longer than the rest should not be competing with them. I have shown what light I can with a number of controversial editorials. With Chris I could do much more. (46)

But Chris has his own valid reasons not to respond promptly and positively to the call of Ikem, although at that stage of their association, H. E. was not 'a monster' (46) as yet. Ikem is also convinced that the "intellectual playfulness displayed by Sam must be less dangerous than the joyless passion for power of many African tyrants." (50)

But, Sam continues to nurse a grievance against the Abazonians and Ikem as the latter hails from this province. Sam suspects the role of both Ikem and Chris for the oppostion to him. It is driven home to him conveniently by Okong. Larry Diamond in his Review Essay on *Anthills of the Savannah*, succinctly sums up the behaviour of a dictator relying on the questionable loyalty of his sycophants. He observes:

> We see in this portait a dictator becoming obsessed with power and the need for absolute and total loyalty to himself, intolerant of the slightest opposition or criticism, and suspicious of plots against him. Isolated from the free flow of information, power loses both perspective and accountability, retreating into a narrow circle of lackeys and flatterers. The theme is old but timeless: power unchecked feeds on itself, becomes intoxicated with itself, and seeks

relentlessly to aggrandize itself.[8]

Larry Diamond's analysis with reference to the evil side of power vis-a-vis its practitioners, and the "narrow circle of lackeys" is striking at once as a universal phenomenon which we all see day in and day out in our own small establishments or places of work.

Sam makes no secrets of his suspicion and contempt for Chris when the former shows his indignation by saying: "It's you, my old friends, you and Ikem who swore for reasons best known to you to force a show-down." (143) What has been a battle of nerves or cold-war so far between friends surfaces as 'a show-down' with no prospects whatsoever for a possible retrieval of the old intimacy and values. Sam allows himself to be guided by suspicion and imagines ghosts where none exist.

Around this time, Sam happens to participate in a meeting of the OAU attended by several African Heads of States. Sam, the socialite, returns home transformed into a state of "seclusion to prepare his own face and perfect his act." (53) He distances himself consciously from his friends. Consequently, he relies more and more for advice, guidance and security on the Director, SRC (State Research Council, comparable to RAW in India and such corresponding secret police services in any modern state) and the Chief of Army, whom he claims with a sense of pride as his own personal choice.

Ikem's crusading editorial pleading for a ban on capital punishment in the wake of getting the convicts executed by a firing-squad on a specially erected venue for this purpose in full view of people, who look at the monstrous exercise as a kind of celebration, is promptly accepted by Sam. Thereafter, he bans capital punishment. However, the credit for it is not conceded to Ikem, but taken by Sam himself. As the four convicts were done to death for different charges including thefts, robbery and the like, Ikem's thoughts turned on the so-called leaders "who openly looted our treasury, whose effrontery soiled our national soul." (42) However, for Chris, Ikem is a kind of "anarchic free spirit" and "refuses to be pinned down by his responsibilities . . . or by the realities of power."[9]

Beatrice points out the weak spots in Ikem's sensibility with reference to his understanding of women whom he considers as mere 'comforters.' His views on women largely fit into the pattern of patriarchy and male domination. His affair with and treatment of Elewa, his girl-friend, tend to portray him as anti-feminist. His revolutionary thinking almost excludes women from its purview. But, ultimately, his association with Beatrice brings about a transformation in his image of woman. He acknowledges sincerely before her that he owes to her "the gift of insight" (96) into a proper understaning of women.

III

Women in Achebe's first three novels are hardly assigned any role worth mentioning and their image as individuals remains dwarfed in a polygamous and patriarchal set up. *A Man of the People* marks a radical departure from this dwarfed image of woman. Eunice in this novel emerges as a strong feminist and participates actively in the political events of the novel. She alone displays enough courage to avenge the death of her lover, Max, by killing the culprit herself. But these incidents happen at the fag-end of the novel without leaving much scope for a proper development or progression in the character of Eunice.

Achebe decries the damned image of woman as depicted in the Bible, Eve in particular, in terms of a Temptress and as one responsible for the fall of Man. He observes: "The original oppression of Woman was based on crude denigration. She caused Man to fall. So she became a scapegoat." (97) This image of woman with minor variations seems to be a familiar feature in many a holy scripture representing different religions. Manu's version of woman needing to be protected all along her life—from girlhood to old age under the care of a father, a husband and a son at different stages of her existence—is hardly conducive for the proper growth of a woman's personality. The system of polygamy legitimized by the tradition in Africa and the Islamic religion and law reduce woman to a child-bearing machine.

Beatrice in *Anthills of the Savannah* enjoys not only a positive image but she does things which the tradition has enjoined on man. According to Chidi Ikonne, the novel "embodies [through Beatrice] Achebe's most positive image of the modern woman in his novels so far."[10] She introduces herself: "My name is Beatrice, but most of my friends call me either B or B.B." (83) Her introduction by H.E. himself to the privileged guests at the Abichi Retreat (President's Guest House) is as follows:

> this is one of the most brilliant daughters of this country. Beatrice Okoh. She is a Senior Assistant Secretary in the Ministry of Finance—the only person in the service, male or female, with a first class honours in English. And not from a local University but from Queen Mary College, University of London. . . . We are proud of her. (75)

Her name at baptism is "Nwanyibuife—a female is also something." (87) Her birth is not marked by gaiety or enthusiasm as she happened to be a fifth girl in a row. That the fifth issue should also turn out to be a girl disappointed her parents, her mother in particular.

Beatrice is very sensitive, shrewd and capable of visualising the course of events to happen. She also earns the image of 'a priestess' and 'a goddess' by Ikem and Chris respectively. But she prefers the image of a 'prophetess-cum-priestess' like Chielo in *Things Fall Apart*. According to David Carroll, "she is the most ambitious creation in the novel" [11] and she combines in herself "both the worlds of modern politics and . . . ancient myth."[12]

Beatrice tells Chris (whom she loves and hopes to marry) that Ikem resents him for his passivity in matters of state and his association with Sam. She also warns him well in advance that both of them (Ikem and Chris) are in trouble and prevails on Chris that he must patch up with Ikem by sorting out all his problems. Later on, she reiterates her apprehensions about the lurking danger to all of them including herself following her brief encounter with "the power brokers" at the Holiday Resort of H. E. She says: "And I see trouble building up for us. It will get to Ikem first. No joking, Chris. He will be the precursor to make straight the way. But after him it will be you. We are all in it, Ikem, you, me and even him. The thing is no longer a joke." (114-15) Her prophetic prediction almost comes true except that she alone survives the tragedy to carry on the work left unfinished by Ikem and Chris. Her understanding of people; her assesment of events; and her incisive insight into future bear testimony to her dual image of both a priestess and prophetess.

Like her fellow "been-tos," Beatrice is also alienated from her roots, traditions, native myths and legends. But she is restored to all these following her humiliation, a kind of reversal of "bottom power" (84) at the Retreat. She happens to be a special invitee—the only one of her kind representing buracracy—sharing the company of VIPs of Kangan, rather "the new power-brokers around his excellency!" (76) She feels ill-at-ease in the company of this "drab group" of invitees—eight men and seven women in all—"chosen on pathetically incompetent advice to impress the American girl" (76) journalist, Miss Cranford, the star-guest at dinner. Apart from some Cabinet Ministers (minus Chris), the group comprised Major Johnson Ossai, Director, SRC, who behaves like "some kind of superior steward," and the Chief of Army, General Lango.

Beatrice feels atrocious that the American girl-journalist should address both the Director, SRC, and the Chief of Army by their first names. The way she takes liberty with H.E. is no less outrageous. She seems to have been invited to provide "the woman's angle" (75) to the American girl and to sort out the problems "between two old friends," Chris and Sam (even in the absence of one of them) in addition to do her turn in Sam's bed. Chris's comment before she left home for Abichi comes alive. He says to Beatrice on phone: "He [Sam] knows things are now pretty hopeless and may see in you a last hope to extricate himself. You may be able to help." (173)

Beatrice, indeed, is a ray of hope not only for Sam but for others as well. After drinks and dinner, she is summoned to do her turn in the bed-chamber of Sam (probably after the American girl). She narrates in poignant terms how she is disgraced. "I did it shamelessly. I cheapened myself. God! I did it to your glory like the dancer in a Hindu temple. Like Esther, oh yes like Esther for my long suffering people." (81) She finds herself reduced to a kind of Devadasi meant to fulfil the lust of a feudal lord.

Beatrice earns the rebuke of "a racist" from Sam as she tries to tease him saying whether such a thing is possible at the White House of Washington where the President of the United States could be held a hostage by an alien girl. Sam is enraged and she is immediately despatched home well past mid-night. She resents strongly the way she was invited to the dinner on behalf of H.E.; the manner of her being whisked away to a distance of forty odd miles; the security search on her before she could be sent inside; Sam's repulsive behaviour with her; her final disgrace in his chamber; and above all, her unceremonious ejection from the "Retreat" at the dead of night. She wonders what sort of "Retreat" is the Presidential Holiday resort on which huge sums of money were spent both by the former civilian government and the present military regime. The pertinent query regarding the Retreat is:

> 'Retreat from what? From whom?' I recall him demanding with characteristic heat. 'From the people and their basic needs of water which is free from Guinea worm, of simple shelter and food. That's what you are retreating from. You retreat up the hill and commune with your cronies and forget the very people who legitimize your authority.' (73)

It is a shame and disgrace that those in power are allowed to neglect the basic needs of people and run away from the very people who "legitimize their authority."

Beatrice unburdens all her anguish and wrath on Chris who visits her leisurely on the following day. She resents his advice before she left for Abichi to 'keep all options open.' (73) While "Christopher prides on his detachment, his cool reasonableness; those . . . very qualities . . . irritate and distress Beatrice.[13]

Beatrice is brought home late in the night 'tired and disgraced.' She sleeps well for some time but wakes up intermittently. Strangely enough, she hears the unusual chirping and songs of birds on the trees in the

Government Reserved Area of her apartment. It turns out to be a thrilling experience as she is not used to this phenomenon, being a habitual late riser. She sat up in her bed listening to the bird's song and recollects through nostalgia how her mother would decode for her the meaning of the birds' song and their mission as the unpaid guards of the king's treasury. The bird's song implies: "Is the king's property correct?" (108) The song is reiterated several times so as to alert the guards on duty. The message of the song moves Beatrice and touches the very core of her being and tears well up in her eyes. She responds to the bird's call by saying: "Poor fellow. You have not heard the news? The king's treasury was broken into last night and all his property carried away—his crown, his sceptre and all." (108) Her unhappy experience at the Retreat signifies her deflowering and her disgrace. The bird's song acted as a balm to the disturbed psyche of Beatrice. The bird's song helps her renew her contact with her roots and the legends of the land from which she is alienated and it also quickens the process of her reassimilation into the mainstream of her native tradition, besides restoring her to the history of her country. The bird's song also helps her delineate herself so that she comes into her own old self with a bang. Beatrice's brief association with "the power brokers" at the Retreat helps her grasp to what extent and how badly the power apparatus could be misused. The adage "power corrupts and absolute power corrupts absolutely" is applicable to any system or arrangement where power is involved. Power, like poison and alcohol spreads fast into every part of the body and can intoxicate anybody so as to turn a friend into a foe; an innocuous person into a mini-monster; a saint into a sinner; and a God into a devil. Beatrice rises to the occasion and acts as a catalyst to motivate both Ikem and Chris emboldening them to offer resistance to the naked dance of Power.

IV

Anthills of the Savannah is a critique on the power apparatus in a neo-colonial situation. The novel also serves as an antidote to the ugly march of Power. Achebe tries to accomplish this objective not through the prescription of a class-war, or Fanonist violence, but by means of incessant struggles, the forms of which are embodied in the indigenous myths and legends.

The novelist uses the myth of the Sun (symbolized in Sam) whose power of scorching heat destroys everything around. The destructive nature of the Sun creates a terrible drought in Abazon, forcing its leadership to visit H.E. for the redressal of their problem caused by the drought. The second most powerful myth is related to the Pillar of Water

(Beatrice in the context of the novel) which seeks to put out the fire of the Sun and also quench the thirst of the parched lands (of Abazon). Corruption-prone and monstrous masculine power is sought to be checkmated by Idemili, God's daugher. Achebe succinctly portrays this legend of male-power which is sought to be neutralised through female resistance:

> In the beginning Power rampaged through our world, naked. So the Almighty, looking at his creation through the round undying eye of the Sun, saw and pondered and finally decided to send his daughter, Idemili, to bear witness to the moral nature of authority by wrapping around Power's rude waist a loincloth of peace and modesty. (102)

The twin-myths of the Sun and the Pillar of Water reinforce "Idemili's contempt for man's unquenchable thirst to sit in authority on his fellows." (102) The unrestrained naked dance of Power is sought to be countered by means of struggle motif in the novel. Beatrice passionately pleads with Chris once again to sort out all his problems with Ikem to save the latter from the impending danger to his life. But the sad truth is that Chris himself is in trouble and his position in the Cabinet has already become vulnerable. His dilemma is that he can neither quit his position, nor can he fight from within. He is summoned by H.E. and pressurized to serve orders of suspension on Ikem for the latter's alleged subversive activities. As Chris refuses to comply, H.E. gets the orders of suspension served on Ikem signed by some one else.

Following his suspension from the Gazette, Ikem is determined to fight openly the fascist regime to the last. In this process, he also manages to de-alienate himself paving the way for his reassimilation into the mainstream of his nation's life and its history. He joins the delegation from Abazon at the Presidential Palace. It comprised no more than half a dozen elders of Abazon. But they were also joined by a fairly large crowd of Abazonians living in Bassa (the capital of Kangan). This delegation and the 'motely-crowd' of people send shock-waves to H.E. The unlettered and anonymous leader of the delegation addresses the crowd. His talk is subtly couched in riddles, myths, legends and parables—the very essence of age-old wisdom as embodied in the oral-lore of the land. He begins his talk by saying: "It is proper that a beggar should visit a king. . . . It is the place of the poor man to visit the rich man who holds the yam and the knife." (127) That the very people who legitimize the authority of those in power should be disgraced as beggars is a sad commentary on the nexus between the people and the rulers. The old man also ridicules the idea of Sam wanting to become the President-for-Life. He affirms that there can be no permanent arrangement in the scheme of things. Even a marriage, he opines, becomes null-and-void the moment one of the partners dies.

It seems as if the sixth sense of the old man tells him that H.E. is not likely to respond positively to their sufferings and grievances. He obliquely drops hints exhorting the Abazonians to prepare themselves for yet another "show-down" if it becomes inevitable. His message emphasising on the 'battle,' 'the battle-cry' and the 'story' which alone survives both 'war and warrior' is very striking and significant. He says:

> The sounding of the battle-drum is important; the fierce waging of the war itself is important; and the telling of the story afterwards—each is important in its own way. I tell you there is not one of them we could do without. But if you ask me which of them takes the eagle-feather I will say boldly: the story . . . only the story can continue beyond the war and the warrior. It is the story that outlives the sound of war-drums and the exploits of brave fighters. It is the story, not the others, that saves our progeny from blundering like blind beggars into the spikes of the cactus fence. The story is our escort; without it we are blind. Does the blind man own his escort? No, neither do we the story; rather it is the story that owns us and directs us. (123-24)

The unlettered man's stress on the "story" as the 'escort,' and as a lesson to be learnt from the past experiences is very revealing. 'The story,' in other words, is the history of a people's past, their glorious moments and sufferings, and the record of (oral or written) their heroic resistance to all forms of oppression and exploitation.

The Abazonian elder concludes his talk with a fantastic parable related to the age-old animosity between the leopard and the tortoise. The parable is as follows: the leopard is always on the look out for the tortoise wanting to kill him. When the latter is about to be killed, he pleads with his killer to leave him alone for a minute or two enabling him to prepare himself mentally for his death. The death-wish of the tortoise is generously conceded. Meanwhile, the tortoise begins to kick, rove and throw dust in different directions. The leopard is intrigued at the crazy behaviour of the tortoise and asks the latter if he has something up his sleeve. The tiny animal says: "Because even after I am dead I would want anyone passing by this spot to say, yes, a fellow and his match struggled here." (128) The story-teller is also conscious of the fact that the struggle in the offing between the ruthless state-power and the unarmed beggars like them is uneven and is doomed to be a failure. And yet, the old man insists that the spirit of the struggle has to be kept alive as a living lesson to posterity. He observes as he wound up his talk: "My people, that is all we are doing now. Struggling to no purpose except that those who come after us will be able to say: True, our fathers were defeated but they tried." (128) The old man receives a standing ovation from the assembly of the Abazonians. The old man's talk tremendously influences the thought-processes of the highly-educated Ikem. Folktales, songs, their inventors-cum-performers are considered to be a challenge to state power and its minions. Folk-lore and its performing artists are essentially subversive in terms of their message and mode of conduct.

The kind of response to the old-man's talk and Ikem's presence there are viewed seriously by Sam and his sycophants. Matters precipitate and come to a head-on-collision between state-power and those who are ranged against it. The story-teller and his associates are arrested and thrown behind the bars at the Bassa Maximum Security Prison. Ikem is invited to a function organized by the Bassa University Students' Union on the campus. He titled his lecture: "The Tortoise and the Leopard – a Political Meditation on the Imperative of Struggle" (153).

He began his lecture on a note of sarcasm and said: "story tellers are a threat. They threaten all champions of control, they frighten usurpers of the right-to-freedom of the human spirit – in state, in church or mosque, in party congress, in the university or wherever." (153) The message contained in this passage comes home to us all the more with a much greater relevance as we are a witness to, if not participants in, the sordid drama of struggle between state-power and the organisations ranged against it, albeit their limitations and weaknesses.

Ikem's lecture covers a wide range of topics, events, matters, personalities and state-power. He is critical of the breed of parasites – the university students and the faculty. He indicts the faculty for priding on its parasitism and for their incorrigible habit of parroting the text-book-oriented theories on revolution, Marxism and the like ignoring the functional aspect of it. He seems to be of the view that knowledge of a theory however great and magnificent, suffers seriously in the hands of its pseudo-ideologues (with whom our universities are littered).

Ikem assumes the role of "a sociologist of literature" and observes that in the third-world context, the writers "must not stop at the stage of documenting social problems but move to the higher responsibility of proffering prescriptions." (161) The most vital part of the lecture is his piece of advice to the students (since the faculty in any case is incorrigible) wanting them to "Examine the condition of their lives because . . . the unexamined life is not worth living." Ikem as a poet and a novelist, like Achebe himself, is committed "to widen the scope of that self-examination." (158)

Answering a query after the lecture, Ikem casually reacted to the rumour about Sam's intention to have his image engraved on a coin. He remarked: "My view is that any serving President foolish enough to lay his head on a coin should know he is inciting people to take it off, the head I mean." (162) *The Gazette* under the leadership of a new editor flashed Ikem's lecture as the main story with a sensational caption: "EX-EDITOR ADVOCATES REGICIDE." (162)

In the final phase of the novel, Sam's regime turns fascist and resorts to violence indiscriminately. Ikem's residence is raided and ransacked at the dead of night; he is arrested; put in hand-cuffs and taken away from his place. An official announcement put out a fabricated story that Ikem tried to snatch the gun from his escort and is shot fatally in the altercation. Even his dead body was not handed over to his friends for burial. This marks the fall of the first 'green bottle,' the victim of state-repression. Larry Diamond links up Ikem's murder to

> the real life-murder of *Newswatch* editor Dele Giwa in October 1986. Like the fictional Ikem Osodi, Dele Giwa was a hero to a great many of his countrymen, intellectuals and non-literates alike. Like Ikem, he was a crusader for freedom, accountability and justice, a brash investigator, a fearless and outspoken commentator . . . the similarity between the two men in temperament and political stature, and the considerable suspicion and circumstantial evidence linking Nigeria's state security apparatus to Giwa's murder, leaves one with an eerie feeling of the way life, and death, imitate art.[14]

This is how imaginative literature often bears a close resemblance to life and mirrors the prevalent contemporary situation in authentic terms.

V

Chris leaves his place for good and goes into a hide-out under the escort of the President, Students' Union, Emmanuel, and a leader of the taxi-union, Braimoh. He manages to establish contact with a BBC correspondent and gives the actual version of Ikem's murder in cold-blood. People of Kangan learn about Ikem's death through the foreign media. Chris keeps changing his hide-out fairly frequently to evade the eye of the SRC. Emmanuel manages to publish a news item saying that Chris had left home in disguise by a foreign-airliner. After a week of hide-out in Bassa at different places, they decide to move to Abazon both for reasons of safety and also as a homage to the memory of the martyred Ikem.

On the eve of Chris's departure for Abazon, Beatrice joins him and they spend their last night together sharing the scanty accommodation at Braimoh's place. It was an experience to them as to the horrible living condition of most people living in Bassa. Chris feels sorry that he had not cared to cultivate the student leaders and others earlier. It is evident that a crisis-situation makes them realize the readiness of the common people to join them in their struggle against the fascist regime. It also helps Chris strike roots in his native soil from which he is alienated because of the Western influence and his high-class living.

Chris and his escort decide in favour of public transport and the journey to Abazon begins. The bus stops on the way because of a crowd in a frenzy, celebrating the fall of the military-government at Bassa. People were on a drinking spree emptying bottles of beer and other drinks. A young girl travelling with them by the same bus gets off along with Chris and others. A soldier in uniform tries to molest her. Chris threatens to report him to the higher officials. Chris is shot at point-blank range by the gun-wielding fellow. Lyn Innes, commenting on the heroic action of Chris says: "Chris's final act is significant because he intervenes and acts rather than remaining detached, and also because his intervention is an outraged reaction to the most blatant abuse of male power against a woman."[15] Chris collapses uttering his last words, somewhat incoherently: "The last Grain. . . . A violent cough throttled the rest." (216) There is an element of melodrama about the tragic death of Chris which is attributed to Chance by Sarma. He observes: "it would be a Chance . . . if you survive a Dictator's wrath but still meet with an inglorious death at the hands of a drunken soldier in a totally absurd situation, as it happens to Chris in the novel."[16] Samson in the fashion of his Biblical-counterpart, invites his own doom. He is kidnapped from his Presidential palace, "tortured and shot in the head and buried under one foot in the bush.' (219) Sam's Chief of Army, whom he claimed proudly as his trusted and loyal follower takes over the reins of administration. The Director, SRC, is reported missing with his whereabouts unknown. This is how the triumvirate fall one after the other and are smashed on the floor like three green bottles.

Of the four protagonists, Beatrice, "the last hope," alone survives the tragedy to carry on the unfinished task left behind by both Ikem and Chris. She is left alone to delineate and 'appease' the 'embittered history.' The four characters are clubbed and treated together because Sam, outside power-syndrome, enjoyed an impeccable and a 'virgin' image. His contact and association with power has undone him ultimately. Hence, the reiteration that it is Power who stands out as the real villain, culprit and criminal in the context of the novel. Fall of governments, a kind of fall from "grace to grass" becomes a recurrent feature and appears to be the only certitude in the midst of uncertainty and choas. This is yet another harsh neo-colonial reality.

VI

Beatrice manages to take the tragedy of Chris in her stride gradually. Her "virtual silence" for many weeks is an "eloquent tribute" to her stoic stature. Emmanuel and the girl, Adamma, whom Chris rescues, keep company to Beatrice. She declines the special invitation extended to her by the new Head of State at the state funeral accorded to Chris.

Beatrice decides to conduct the naming ceremony for Ikem – Elewa's daughter in her flat. The father is supposed to do it according to the tradition. She chooses a boy's name for the girl-child. The name chosen is *AMAECHINA; May-the-path never-close*. The name signifies "hope that springs eternal . . . Beatrice chooses for the girl the path of Ikem, the path of struggle . . . of course, of inspiration and of hope."[17] This is Achebe's version of feminism with Beatrice rising to the occasion to discharge the responsibilities assigned to men by tradition.

Thus, the doomed journeys of the "trailed travellers" (both Ikem and Chris) directed by "alienated history" (220) see light at the end of the tunnel. The lead role played by Beatrice; the path shown by Ikem; and the heroic death invited unwittingly by Chris should go a long way "to appease an embittered history" of a people, and at the same time resolve to a large extent, Beatrice's anxiety about the same.

The motif of 'struggle' is the hall-mark of the novel with story as the "escort" and guide. The narrator of the story in this process, "can become a powerful force in shaping the way a people think about their social and political order, and the nature, desirability and direction of change."[18]

Thus, the story of the people's struggle "will stand reincarnated . . . like the scorched anthills of the Savannah both as a warning and a promise."[19] The novel is also a clarion call to struggle, and its story is an existential affirmation of the necessity and dignity of the struggle against evil as an end in itself."[20]

Unlike Ngugi, Achebe does not recommend any alternative forms of governance. Democratic forms of government chipped out of the West Minister model and transplanted in the Third-World countries have left much to be desired. Achebe does not recommend any alternate modes of governance but only struggle and vigil to checkmate the onslaughts of power on human dignity and liberty.

Power or any establishment in whatever form based on a specific ideology breeds corruption from within and without. Democratic rule, dictatorial regimes, theocratic powers, socialist states—all suffer invariably from the power-virus. Hence, *Anthills of the Savannah* could be considered a great political novel with a message. It is a study in post-Marxist dialectics as it seeks to look beyond Marxism.

VII

The title *Anthills of the Savannah* strikes the keynote of the novel's theme. The anthills are the living witness to unfold the recurring cycle of the destruction and regeneration of Savannah "surviving to tell the new grass of the Savannah about last year's bush fires." The story, thus, outlives the event and the writer by narrating the cataclysmic changes in human history leaves it to us to draw the right lessons.

Achebe suggests that any concept of man propounded by philosophers cannot be taken as axiomatic truth. He maintains:

> All certitude must now be suspect. One must develop the habit of scepticism, not swallow every piece of superstition you are told by witch doctors and professors (161).

> The simplistic remedies touted by all manner of salesmen . . . will always fail because of man's stubborn antibody called surprise. Man will surprise by his capacity for nobility as well as villainy. No system can change that. It is built into the core of man's free spirit. (99)

Achebe observes that one can reform society only on the basis of what it is, its core of reality, not on the basis of an intellectual abstraction. To annotate Achebe, man's potential for good or evil is tested on the touchstone of temptation or/and power. Only an ever-vigilant culture of self-restraint and discipline can save the individual and the society from a slide into extremism and anarchy.

Achebe's analysis of the human psyche and his insight into human nature has as its grounding a profound study of contemporary African history. *Anthills* is a scathing indictment of military dictatorship seizing power through violent coups which prove worse than the civilian misrule. The continual pursuit of power without scruples spells disaster to the people who, shorn of all civil liberties, become its worst victims. The untold suffering and misery inflicted on the people throws up leaders like Ikem, Chris and Beatrice who rise in revolt against the tyrannous establishment. They sow the seeds of courage and fortitude in the masses to stand up against the new oppressors. Ikem and Chris face persecution and are eventually liquidated. But they never gave up the struggle. In the fable of the tortoise and the leopard, the tortoise insists on leaving behind the traces of its struggle before getting killed. The likes of Ikem would rather die struggling against the foe than meekly submit to him – preferring death to defeat.

Struggle is the watchword and the precious legacy they leave to posterity. The awakening in the people's consciousness aroused by these martyrs is the only insurance against despotic regimes and their sycophantic cliques.

Achebe does not subscribe to grandiose ideologies either of the left or the right. He denounces regimented policies pursued by the ruling coteries of either party which inevitably degenerates into intrigues and manoeuvring of power politics. Achebe observes: "Orthodoxy whether of the right or the left is the graveyard of creativity." (100) It would be illusory to think that a millenium will dawn one fine day upon humanity ensuring the supremacy of freedom and happiness for everyone once and for all.

According to Achebe, "Experience and intelligence warn us that man's progress in freedom will be piecemeal, slow and undramatic." (99) One has always to strive and struggle, be ever vigilant against new forms of slavery for the creation of a better man and a better society. Beatrice represents the new awakened woman who is a reservoir of great strength and fortitude. She would be companion in arms to man in this continual historic struggle.

NOTES

1. Chinua Achebe, *Anthills of the Savannah* (London: Picador in association with William Heinemann, 1987).
2. Chinua Achebe, *A Man of the People.*
3. T.R.S. Sharma, "*Anthills of the Savannah*: The Problematics of Power/Discourse in the Third World Post-Colonial Context," *Journal of Contemporary Thought* (Delhi: Inaugural issue, 1991), p.125.
4. C.L. Innes, "The Critic as Novelist: *Anthills of the Savannah*," *Chinua Achebe*, p. 150.
5. *Ibid.*, p.125.
6. David Carroll, "*Anthills of the Savannah,*" *Chinua Achebe*, p. 167.

7. *Ibid.,* p.172.
8. Larry Diamond, "Review Essay: Fiction of Political Thought," *African Affairs*, Vol. 88, no. 352 (July 1989), p. 125.
9. Chidi Ikonne, *Anthills of the Savannah*: Book Review in *UFAHMU,* Vol. XVI, no. 3, (Spring 1988), p. 51.
10. David Carroll, *p. 175.*
11. *Ibid.,* pp. 175-76.
12. *Ibid.*
13. C.L. Innes, p. 152.
14. Larry Diamond, p. 437.
15. C.L. Innes, p. 157.
16. T.R.S. Sharma, p. 127.
17. Larry Diamond, p. 445.
18. *Ibid.*, p. 435.
19. David Carroll, p. 185.
20. Larry Diamond, p. 443.

La Luta Continua
(Let the Struggle Continue)
Conclusion

The concluding part of the book seeks to sum up its findings and presents in an abridged form the thematic principle in each chapter. The final section of the chapter is a brief commentary on the relevance and applicability of the commitment of the two writers in the context of post-modernism.

In the African context as it really obtains today, the philosophy of power (i.e., values of welfare state, democracy or socialism) gets bogged down into the politics of power. A sense of insecurity and instability for the ruler(s) degenerate into a psychology of survival at any cost. The lure of power and with it the lure of money and sex breed in the ruling establishment a *hubris* which goes all out to suppress, even eliminate all opposition to it. Failure to strike a proper equation between power, people and good governance, results in the abandoning of all human values. This, in sum, is the tragic scenario of Africa and the entire third-world in the post-independence phase.

Achebe and Ngugi are committed to the political freedom and cultural renaissance of Africa. Both are sadly disillusioned by the post-colonial native regimes—civilian rule or army dictatorship. The hopes and aspirations of the people for a free, prosperous and dignified Africa are belied and betrayed. The ray of hope, in both the writers, inheres in the elightened consciousness of the people and their determination to continue the struggle for a reformed Africa having its pride of place in the comity of nations.

The three novels of Achebe included in the book are a study in the psychology, philosophy and politics of power and how it manifests itself in several ways stampeding and bulldozing human dignity and equality. The ugly and unbridled march of power is sought to be checkmated by means of a sustained struggle against it. Power and struggle sum up the discussion on these novels.

Ngugi's early fiction historicises the heroic resistance to colonial power and his later fiction is concerned with the peoples' liberation struggles against the neo-colonial order. The novelist uses Christian religious symbolism to reinforce the motif of rebellion against the indigenous, corrupt and anti-people regimes. The twin motifs of religion and rebellion explicate the seminal argument on the novels of Ngugi.

The novels of Achebe are predominantly tragic. *Things Fall Apart* and *Arrow of God* deal with the rise and fall of the towering protagonists (Okonkwo and Ezeulu) whose tragic end evokes the empathy of the readers. In *Anthills*, two major protagonists, Ikem and Chris get liquidated as they choose to throw their lot with the people and against the corrupt and authoritarian army rule. However, the novel ends on a note of optimism with the most powerful female protagonist of Achebe (Beatrice) surviving the tragedy to carry on the path of struggle shown by her illustrious associates.

With the exception of *The River Between*, Ngugi's first written novel, all his novels abound in optimism and fit finely into the pattern of socialist realism. Waiyaki, the protagonist in *The River Between*, fails to gauge the depth of people's feelings for the restoration of the lost lands and political freedom. He falls a victim while attempting to reconcile the antagonistic ridges of Kameno and Makuyu.

The multiple protagonists in *A Grain of Wheat* and *Petals of Blood* are involved in a grim battle against the colonial and neo-colonial power cliques. They struggle, suffer and sacrifice in their relentless pursuit and quest for the dawn of a socialist order and egalitarian values. Achebe is also committed to a just order in which everybody, the common man in particular, can live with a sense of equality and dignity. But Achebe would not recommend any particular system or mode of governance. Instead, he pleads for constant vigilance and sustained struggle against all forms of governance. The objectives of Achebe and Ngugi meet and mix in the motif of struggle. Achebe's emphasis on *Amaechina* (Let the path [of struggle] never close) and Ngugi's slogan *La Luta Continua* (Let the struggle continue) embrace and embody the struggle principle to which both the writers are committed.

Achebe's fiction is a bold and brilliant attempt at Africanizing the alien English language and the very genre of fiction—which the Eurocentric writers claim to be their monopoly. He has been able to indigenise the alien language showing the way to the younger generation of writers as to how it could be handled to convey the African experience with an unmistakable African flavour about it. For Ngugi, continued use of English language amounts to the acceptance of and adherence to cultural imperialism. He asserts that elimination of English and its replacement by native African languages is an important and essential step in the direction of decolonizing the mind. It is a necessary measure to decolonize African literature and other areas of human experiences.

II

Achebe's Okonkwo in *Things Fall Apart* is an uncompromising nationalist who is prepared to go all out to oust the white intruder. Although he is proud of his African identity and believes in industry, valour and strength, he lacks in intelligence and wisdom to organise and lead the people against the common alien enemy.

Ezeulu in *Arrow of God* is a leader with a socio-political vision, who while respecting the Igbo tradition and values would like to synthesize them with the benefits of modern education and administration. He hated the white man's arrogance and his superiority complex and would on no account accept or acquiesce in his domination. But his own tribal jealousies engineered by his rival Nwaka, who succeeds in the assembly by overruling Ezeulu at critical points, get the better of his judgement when he chooses to exercise his power as priest to deprive and punish his own people by delaying the harvesting operations. The temptation to use power as priest, which is his own sole prerogative, makes him go against the people's interests and fall an unwitting victim to the white man's designs.

The post independent disenchantment with native rule reflected in *A Man of the People* grows manifold with the military dictator, Sam in *Anthills of the Savannah*. Sam represents the victory of evil over good totally betraying people's trust and confidence. The novel shows how evil triumphs by using adroitly "Good" as its instrument. His lip service to ideals and values is like the devil quoting scriptures, exposing in the process "the smiling face of Mephistopheles in the beguiling habit of a monk." Ikem and Chris are the sincere standard bearers of freedom who finally disassociate themselves from the abominable power apparatus and eventually fall martyrs to the cause of the people.

In a searching analysis of the psychology of power, Achebe warns against its traps and pitfalls and the tendency to overcome them by easy presumptions and quick solutions. One has to reckon with human weaknesses and frailties in succumbing to the temptation of power whatever be the nature of establishment. The powers that be need to have vital links with the people at the grassroots and the people in their turn require to be ever alert and active in their struggle for freedom from newer forms of bondage. In the final analysis, only an ever-vigilant culture of self-restraint and discipline can save the individual and the society from a slide into extremism and anarchy.

Ngugi is a committed writer and believes in class war and in the seizure of political power by workers and peasants through violent struggles. He is an uncompromising champion of African identity and culture and pleads for the decolonization of mind from all traces of subservience and enslavement that smack of the white man's hegemony in areas of culture, language, Eurocentred values, capitalistic, imperialistic, economic and political domination.

In *The River Between*, Ngugi attempts to unify and consolidate the forces of nationalism. Waiyaki, the protagonist, works for a synthesis between the positive features of Kameno and Makuyu. He opposes the white invasion which dispossess the natives of their lands by white settlers disinheriting them from their cultural roots. He, however, does not have the organising capacity to rally the native forces under the banner of anti-colonial struggle. He is a messianic idealist figure who lacks in political acumen and ultimately falls a victim to the selfish designs of another tribal Chieftain.

The distinctive feature in the struggle for freedom is Ngugi's use of Christian religion in reinforcing rebellion against the corrupt establishment. The religious dimension in *A Grain of Wheat* is oriented to the socialist principle. There is an element of what we now call liberation theology in the utterances of Kihika who refuses to take a narrow, dogmatic view of organised Christianity. Kihika uses religious symbolism to effect a change in the status-quo towards realizing humanistic values and socialistic goals.

Ngugi's *Petals of Blood* is also concerned with the issues of corruption and betrayal of people's aspirations in the post-independence phase by the native leadership. Religious symbolism is evoked in the novel as a complementary force to reinforce the motif of rebellion for the establishment of egalitarian values. This particular aspect has not been adequately explored by critics. The novel inaugurates and endorses the era of peoples' liberation struggles in Africa and recommends a socialist order as the only panacea for all the maladies in Africa. Karega, the trade-union protagonist in the novel, shows the path of people's liberation struggles and Joseph, the orphan boy, who turns into "a tall-youth" is also committed to the struggle motif. *Petals of Blood* is rightly hailed as a socialist and the first proletarian African novel.

III

While Achebe is concerned with the loss of human values and dignity due to exploitation of man by man, Ngugi is committed to a socialist order for the resolution of this crisis. Many people including progressive intellectuals are sceptical about the validity and relevance of socialist values in the wake of the disintegration of Socialist powers in East European countries and the U.S.S.R. and in the context of post-modernism. Marxist thinkers and party-liners lost no time to disown and denounce the fallen comrades in terms of revisionists and as apologists to socialism. But the point is that any sytem of governance has an evil side to it in the sense that it breeds corruption, favouritism and the like.

Achebe's fiction, the three selected novels in particular, demonstrate convincingly how the power apparatus degenerates and what needs to be done to checkmate the ugly march of power. The antidote to power, according to Achebe, is the motif of struggle which can effectively counter it (power). The novelist dwells at length on this aspect of the problem emphasising on the forms of struggle and their new modes of application in different contexts corresponding to the changing shapes of neo-colonialism. It is in this perspective that the fiction of Achebe comes alive and becomes relevant.

Ngugi affirms that "the wretched of the earth" cannot be expected to remain subdued and silent for ever and they are bound to wage decisive battles against any oppressive order. Ever-widening and glaring inequalities among people in different parts of the world; a sense of solidarity among the oppressed and their awareness as to their combined strength—constitute a potential source for the rise of rebellion and revolutions. It is in this context that a continual struggle for socialist values becomes relevant. Ngugi is committed on the side of the people in their liberation struggles for "a communal home" to be built on a new foundation.

Things fall apart; cultures crumble; and civilizations disintegrate while history marches ahead taking all these events in its stride. A third-world writer, Achebe avers, has a responsibility not only to document these cataclysmic changes in human history, but even proffer solutions from a proper perspective. This is how a writer can motivate and guide people in order to involve them in a continual struggle so as to make their political freedom more meaningful, functional and relevant. The writings of Achebe and Ngugi are a sincere endeavour in this direction.

BIBLIOGRAPHY

PRIMARY SOURCES

CHINUA ACHEBE

A. NOVELS

Things Fall Apart. London:Heinemann, 1958.
No Longer at Ease. London: Heinemann, 1960.
Arrow of God. London: Heinemann, 1964.
A Man of the People. London: Heinemann, 1966.
Anthills of the Savannah. London: Picador, 1987.

B. SHORT FICTION

The Sacrificial Egg and Other Short Stories. Onitsha: Etudo, 1962.
Girls at War and Other Stories, 1972.

C. NON-FICTION

Morning Yet on Creation Day: Essays. London: Heinemann, 1975.
The Trouble With Nigeria. Enugu: Fourth Dimension, 1983.
Hopes and Impediments: Selected Essays, 1965-87. London: Heinemann, 1988.
Nigerian Essays. Ibadan: Heinemann, 1988.

D. POETRY

Beware Soul Brother and Other Poems. Enugu: Nwankwo-Ifejika, 1971.

E. ARTICLES

"Amos Tutuola," *Radio Times*, 23-29, July 1961, 15.
"Introduction to Delphine King," *Dreams Of Twilights: A Book of Poems*. Apapa: Nigerian National Press, 1962. 5.
"A Look at West African Writing," *Spear* (June 1963), 26.
"On Janheinz Jahn and Ezekiel Mphahlele," *Transition*, 8 (1960), 9.
"The Role of the Writer in a New Nation," *Nigerian Libraries,* I, 3 (1964), 113-19.
Foreword to *A Selection of African Prose*, vol. 1, ed. W.H. Whiteley. Oxford: Clarendon Press, 1964. vii-x.
"The African Writer and the English Language," *Transition*, IV, 8 (1965), 27-30.
"The Black Writer's Burden," *Presence Africaine,* vol. 31, no. 59 (1966), 135-40.
"Contemporary Literature," *The Living Culture of Nigeria*. London: Nelson, 1976.
"African Writing and the Problem of Translation," *Translation*, 3 (1976), 38-43.
"Commitment and the African Writer," *Readings in African Humanities: Cultural Development,* ed. Ogbu U. Kalu. Enugu: Fourth Dimension, 1978. 181-87.
"The Uses of African Literature," *Okike*, 15 (1979), 8-17.

F. INTERVIEWS

Agetua, John. "Interview with Professor Chinua Achebe, August 16, 1976," *Critics on Chinua Achebe 1970-76*. Benin City: 1977.
Baugh, Lawrence E. "An Interview with Chinua Achebe," *Drum* (Amherst), vol. 5, no.3 (1974), 18-22.
Cott, Jonathan, ed. "Chinua Achebe: At the Crossroads," *Pipers at the Gates of Dawn: The Wisdom of Children's Literature.* New York: McGraw Hill, 1985, 161-92.
Duerden, Dennis and Cosmo Pieterse, eds. "Chinua Achebe," *African Writers Talking: A*

Collection of Radio Interviews. New York: Africana Publishing Corp., 1972. 3-17.

Emenyonu, Ernest and Pat Emenyonu. "Achebe: Accountable to Our Society," *Africa Report*, vol. 17, no. 5 (1972), 21, 23, 25-27.

Evalds, Victoria K. "An Interview with Chinua Achebe," *Studies in Black Literature*, vol. 8, no. 1 (1977), 16-20.

Felton, M. "An Interview with Chinua Achebe," *Spectrum: A Magazine of Peace Corps Nigeria*, I, 1 (1967), 4-7.

Hall, Tony. "I Had to Write on the Chaos I Foresaw, " *Sunday Nation*, 15 (January 1967), 5-16.

Hayes, Suzanne. "An Interview with Chinua Achebe (Adelaide 1980)," *New Literatures in English Review*, 11 (n.d.),

Kitchen, Paddy. "A Relevant Art: Paddy Kitchen Talks to Chinua Achebe," *Times Educational Supplement*, 14 April 1972, 19.

Lawson, William. "Chinua Achebe in New England: An Interview," *Yardbird Reader*, 4 (1975), 99-110.

Lindfors, Bernth, *et al*, "Interview with Chinua Achebe," *Palaver: Interview with Five African Writers in Texas*. Austin: African and Afro-American Research Institute, 1972. 5-12.

___. "Achebe on Commitment and African Writers," *Africa Report*, XV, 3 (1970), 16-18.

Morell, Karen L., ed. "Class Discussion," *In Person: Achebe, Awoonor, and Soyinka at the University of Washington*. Seattle: African Studies Program, Institute for Comparative and Foreign Area Studies, University of Washington, 1975. 24-32.

Nksoi, Lewis. "Conversation with Chinua Achebe," *Africa Report*, IX, 7 (1964), 19-21.

Nwachukwu-Agbadu, J.O.J. "Interview with Chinua Achebe," *Massachusetts Review*, vol. 28, no. 2 (Summer 1987), 273-85.

Ogbaa, K. "Interview with Chinua Achebe," *Research in African Literatures*, 12 (Spring 1981), 1-13.

Rutherford, Anna. "Interview with Chinua Achebe," *Kunapipi*, vol. 9, no. 2 (1987), 1-7.

Serumaga, Robert. "Chinua Achebe Interviewed by Robert Serumaga," *Cultural Events in Africa*, 28 (1967), i-vi.

Smith, Michael and Harry Cowen. "*A Man of the People*: Interview with Chinua Achebe," *McGill Report*, 23 (February 1970), 1-2.

Wilmer, Valerie. "Chinua Achebe and the African Novel," *Flamingo*, vol. 4, no. 11 (1965), 27-29.

NGUGI WA THIOG'O

A. NOVELS

Weep Not, Child. London: Heinemann, 1964.

The River Between. London: Heinemann, 1965.

A Grain of Wheat. London: Heinemann, 1967.

Petals of Blood. London: Heinemann, 1977.

Devil on the Cross. London: Heinemann, 1982.

Matigari. London: Heinemann, 1986.

B. SHORT FICTION

Ngugi wa Thiong'O. *Secret Lives*. London: Heinemann, 1975.

C. NON-FICTION

Barrel of a Pen: Resistance to Repression in Neo-Colonial Kenya. New York: African World Press, 1983.

Decolonising the Mind. The Politics of Language in African Literature. London: James Cur-

rey, 1986.
Detained, A Writer's Prison Diary. London: Heinemann, 1981.
Homecoming. London: Heinemann, 1972.
Writers in Politics. London: Heinemann, 1981.
African Literature. London: James Currey, 1986.

D. PLAYS
The Black Hermit. London: Heinemann, 1968.
The Trial of Dedan Kimathi. London: Heinemann, 1976. Co-authored with Micere Githae Mugo.
I will Marry When I Want. London: Heinemann, 1982. Co-authored with Ngugi wa Mirii.

E. ARTICLES
"Education for a National Culture," *UFAHAMU*, XII, 2 (1983), 20-34.
"Life in a Village: Memories of Childhood," *The Writer in Modern Africa*, ed. Per Wastberg. Stockholm: African-Scandinavian Writers' Conference, 1967. 99-107.
"The Language of African Literature," *New Left Review*, (1985), 109-27.

SECONDARY SOURCES

General Studies about African Literature:

A. BOOKS
Agovi, K.E. *Novels of Social Change*. Tema: Ghana Publishing Corporation, 1988.
Amuta, Chidi. *The Theory of African Literature: Implications for Practical Criticism*. London: Zed Books, 1989.
Anniah Gowda, H.H., ed. *The Colonial and Neo-Colonial Encounters in Commonwealth Literature*. Mysore: Prasaranga University of Mysore, 1983.
Bennett, George. *Kenya: A Political History*. Oxford: Oxford University Press, 1963.
p'Bitek, Okot. *Africa's Cultural Revolution*. Nairobi: Macmillan Books for Africa, 1973.
Booth, J. *Writers and Politics in Nigeria*. London: Hodder, 1981.
Brett, E.A. *Colonialism and Underdevelopment in East Africa*. London: Heinemann, 1973.
Chinweizu, *et al. Towards the Decolonization of African Literature*. London: KPI, 1980.
Cook David. *African Literature: A Critical View*. Harlow: Longman, 1977.
Dathorne, O.R. *African Literature in the Twentieth Century*. Minneapolis: University of Minnesota Press, 1975.
Davidson, Basil. *Africa in Modern History*. Harmondsworth: Penguin, 1978.
___. *The People's Cause: A History of Guerrillas in Africa*. London: Longman, 1981.
Dilly, M. *British Policy in Kenya Colony*. London: Cas, 1966.
Diop, David. *Hammer Blows and other Writings*. Bloomington: Indiana University Press 1973.
Emenyonu, Ernest and C.D. Narasimhaiah., eds. *African Literature Comes of Age*. Mysore: Dhvanyaloka, 1988.
Evans, P. *Law and Disorder*. London: Secker and Warburg, 1956.
Fanon, Frantz. *The Wretched of the Earth*. Harmondsworth: Penguin, 1967.
Finnegan, Rooth. *Oral Literature in Africa*. Oxford: Oxford Univ. Press, 1980.
Forde, D. and G.I. Jones. *The Ibo and Ibibio-Speaking Peoples of South-Eastern Nigeria*. London: International African Institute, 1950.
Gubelberger, George M. *Marxism and African Literature*. London: James Currey, 1985.
Ingham, Kenneth. *A History of East Africa*. London: Longam, 1965.
Isichei, E.A. *A History of the Igbo People*. London: Macmillan, 1976.
JanMohamed, Abdul R. *Manichean Aesthetics: The Politics of Literature in Colonial Africa*.

Amherst MA: University of Massachusetts Press, 1983.
Jones, Eldred. "The Decolonization of African Literature," *The Writer in Modern Africa*, ed. per Wastberg. Uppsala: SIAS, 1968. 71.
Karimi, J and P. Ochiend. *The Kenyatta Succession.* Nairobi: Transafrica, 1980.
Kariuki, J.M. *Mau Mau Detainee*. Oxford: Oxford Univ. Press, 1963.
Kenyatta Jomo. *Facing Mount Kenya*. Mercury Books Edition, 1961.
___. *Suffering Without Bitterness*. Nairobi: East African Publishing House, 1961.
Lambert, H.E. *Kikuyu Social and Political Institutions*. Oxford: Oxford University Press, 1956.
Larson, C.R. *The Emergence of African Fiction*. Bloomington: Indiana Univ. Press, 1972.
Leys, Colin. *Underdevelopment in Kenya*. London: Heinemann, 1975.
Lindfors, Bernth. *Early Nigerian Literature*. New York: African Publishing Co., 1982.
Mahood, M.M. *The Colonial Encounter*. London: Rex Collings, 1977.
Majdalany, F. *State of Emergency*. London: Longman, 1962.
Mazuri, Ali A. "The Patriot as an Artist," *African Writers on African Writing*, ed. G.D. Killam. London: Heinemann, 1973. 73-90.
Mboya, Tom. *Freedom and After*. London: Andre Deutsch, 1963.
Meyers, Jeffrey. *Fiction and Colonial Experience*. Ipswich: Boydell Press, 1972.
Middleton, John. *The Kikuyu and Kamba of Kenya*. London: International African Institute, 1953.
Moore, Gerald. *Seven African Writers*. London: Oxford Univ. Press, 1962.
Murray, Pauli. "The Liberation of Black Women," *Women: A Feminist Perspective,* ed. Jo Freeman. California: Mayfield Publishing Co., 1975. 351-63.
Nyerere, Julius K. "Ujamaa—The Basis of African Socialism," *East-West African Literature*, ed. Arne Zehersten. London: Longman, 1983, 168-75.
Ogot, B.A. and J.A. Kieran. *Zamani: A Survery of East African History*. Nairobi: Longmans ofEast Africa/East African Publishing House, 1968.
Ogbalu, F. Chidozie and E. Nolue Emenanjo. *Igbo Language and Culture*. Ibadan: Oxford University Press, 1975.
Oliver, R and G. Mathew, eds. *History of East Africa*, vol. 1. Oxford: Clarendon Press, 1963.
Oldele, Taiwo. *Culture and the Nigerian Novel*. London: Macmillan, 1982.
Peter, Nazareth. *An African view of Literature*. London: Routledge, 1985.
Prins, A.H.J. *East African Age-Class Systems*. Westport: Negro Universities Press, 1970.
Rodrigues, Reinhild. *Unabhangige religiose Bewegungen in Kenia*. Freiburg: Johannes Krause, 1975.
Roscoe, A. *Mother is God: A Study in West African Literature*. London: Cambridge Univ. Press, 1971.
Senghor, Leopold Sedar. *Prose and Poetry*. Trans. John Reed and Clive Wake. London: Heinemann, 1976.
Soyinka, Wole. *Myth, Literature and the African World*. Cambridge: Cambridge Univ. Press, 1976.
Tucker, Forres. *Modern Commonwealth Literature*. New York: Frederick Unger, 1977.
Wasserman, Garry. *Politics of Decolonization*. Cambridge: Cambridge University Press, 1967.

B. ARTICLES

Akinola, Anthony A. "Nigeria: The Quest for a Stable Polity Another Comment," *African Affairs*, vol. 87, no. 348 (July 1988), 441-45.
Amuta, Chidi. "Criticism, Ideology and Society: The Instance of Nigerian Literature," *UFAHAMU*, XII, 2 (1983), 116-37.
Bassey, Celestine O. "Retrospects and Prospects of Political Stability in Nigeria," *African Studies Review*, vol. 32, no. 1 (1989), 97-113.

Comas, James. "The Presence of Theory/Theorizing the Present," *Research in African Literature*, vol. 21, no. 1 (Spring 1990), 5-31.

Diamond, Larry. "Fiction as Political Thought," *African Affairs*, vol. 88, no. 352 (July 1989), 435-45.

Harrow, Kenneth W. "A Formal Approach to African Literature," *Research in African Literature*, vol. 21, no. 1 (Spring 1990), 79-89.

Kinyatti, Maina-wa. "Mau Mau: The Peak of Political Organization and struggle for Liberation in Colonial Kenya," *UFAHAMU*, XII, 3 (1983), 90-123.

Ravenscroft, Arthur. "African Literature V: Novels of Disillusion," *Journal of Commonwealth Literature*, 6 (January 1969), 120-37.

Studies about Achebe and Ngugi

A. BOOKS/ANTHOLOGIES

Abrahams, Cecil A. "George Lamming and Chinua Achebe: Tradition and the Literary Chroniclers," *Awakened Conscience: Studies in Commonwealth Literature*, ed. C.D. Narasimhaiah, New Delhi: Sterling, 1978, 294-306.

Awoonor, Kofi. "James Ngugi, Ferdinand Oyono and the Anti-Colonial Novel," *The Breast of the Earth*. Enugu: NOK Publishers, 1975, 281-305.

Baldwin, W. *Mau Mau Manhunt*. New York: E.P. Dutton, 1975.

Barnett, Donald L. and Karari Nijama. *Mau Mau from Within*. New York: Modern Reader Paperback. 1970.

Brown, Lloyd W. "Cultural Norms and Modes of Perception in Achebe's Fiction," *Research in African Literatures*, 3, (1972), 21-35.

Carroll, David. *Chinua Achebe*. London: Macmillan, 1980.

Cook, David and Michael Okenimkpe. *Ngugi wa Thoing'o: An Exploration of His Writings*. London: Heinemann, 1983.

Coussy, Denise. *L'Oeurve de Chinua Achebe*. Paris: Presence Africaine, 1985.

Dhar, T.N. "Private Dreams and Public Pressures: Ngugi's *Weep Not, Child* and *The River Between, Commonwealth Fiction*, II, ed. R.K. Dhawan, New Delhi: Prestige, 1988, 220-33.

Echeruo, M.J.C. "Chinua Achebe," *A Celebration of Black African Writing*, ed. Bruce King and Kolawole Ogungbesan. Zaria and Ibadan: Ahmadu Bello University Press and Oxford University Press, 1975, 150-63.

Evans, Jennifer. "Mother Africa and the Heroic Whore: Female Images in *Petals of Blood*," *Contemporary Literature*, ed. Hal Wylie, et. al. Washington: Three Continents Press, 1983, 57-65.

Gachukia, Eddah W. "Chinua Achebe and Tradition," *Standpoints on African Literature: A Critical Anthology*, ed. Chris L. Wanjala. Nairobi, Kampala, Dar es Salaam: East African Literature Bureau, 1973, 172-87.

Gakwandi, Shatto Arthur. *The Novel and Contemporary Experience in Africa*. London: Heinemann, 1977.

Gikandi, Simon. *Reading the African Novel*. London: James Currey, 1987, 149-70.

___. "On Cultures and the State: The Writings of Ngugi wa Thiong'o," *Third World Quarterly*, vol. 11, no. 1 (Jan. 1989), 148-56.

Henderson, Ian. *The Hunt for Kimathi*, London: Hamilton, 1964.

Higo, Aigboje. "Introduction," in *Chinua Achebe, Things Fall Apart*. London: Heinemann, 1965. 5-12.

Howard, W.J. "Themes and Development in the Novels of Ngugi," *The Critical Evaluation of African Literature*, ed. Edgar Wright. London: Heinemann, 1973.

Innes, C.L. *Chinua Achebe*. Cambridge: Cambridge Univ. Press. 1990.

___. *Chinua Achebe's Arrow of God: A Critical View*, ed. Yolande Cantu, London: Collins in Association with the British Council, 1985.

___, and B. Lindfors., eds. *Critical Perspectives on Chinua Achebe*. Washington DC.: Three Continents Press, 1978.

___. *The Devil's Own Mirror*. Washington: Three Continents Press, 1990.

Jones, Eldred D., ed. *African Literature Today*. London: Heinemann, 1972.

Killam, G.D. *An Introduction to the Writing of Ngugi*: London: Heinemann, 1980.

___. *The Writings of Chinua Achebe*. London: Heinemann, 1977.

___. "Notions of Religion, Alienation and Archetype in *Arrow of God*," *Exile and Tradition: Studies in African and Caribbean Literature*, ed. Rowland Smith, London: Longman, 1976, 152-65.

Lindfors, Bernth. "*Petals of Blood* as Popular Novel," *Contemporary Literature*, ed. Hal Wylie, et. al. Washington: Three Continents Press, 1983, 49-55.

___. "Chinua Achebe and the Nigerian Novel," *Studies on Modern Black-African Literature*, ed. Pal Paricsy, Budapest: Center for Afro-Asian Research of the Hungarian Academy of Sciences, 1971, 29-49.

___, and Kothandaraman, Bala, ed., *South Asian Responses to Chinua Achebe*. New Delhi: Prestige, 1993.

Mangalam Brown, David. *Land, Freedom and Fiction: History and Ideology in Kenya*. London: Zed Books, 1985.

Moore, Gerald. *The Chosen Tongue*. London: Longman, 1969.

___. "Chinua Achebe: Nostalgia and Realism," *Twelve African Writers*. London: Hutchinson University Press, 1980.

Mphaheele, Ezekiel. *The African Image*. London: Faber and Faber, 1962.

Nandakumar, Prema. "Chinua Achebe," *The Glory and the Good: Essays on Literature*. London: Asia, 1965, 285-304.

Ngara, Emmanuel. *Art and Ideology in the African Novel*. London: Heinemann, 1985.

___. *Stylistic Criticism and the African Novel*. London: Heinemann, 1982.

Ngugi wa Thiong'o "Chinua Achebe: *A Man of the People,*" *Homecoming: Essays on Africa and the Caribbean Literature, Culture and Politics*. London: Heinemann, 1972.

Njoki, Benedict Chiak. *The Four Novels of Chinua Achebe: A Critical Study*. New York: Lang, 1984.

Obiechina, Emmanuel. *Culture, Tradition and Society in the West African Novel*. Cambridge: Cambridge University Press, 1975.

Odinga, Oginga. *Not Yet Uhuru*. London: Heinemann, 1967.

Palmer, Eustace. *The Growth of the African Novel*. London: Heinemann, 1979.

___. *An Introduction to the African Novel*. London: Heinemann, 1972.

Peters, Jonathan A. *A Dance of Masks: Senghor, Achebe and Soyinka*. Washington: Three Continents Press, 1978.

Pieterse, Cosmos and Dennis Duerden. *African Writers Talking*. London: Heinemann, 1973.

Povey, John. "The Novels of Chinua Achebe," *Introduction to Nigerian Literature*, ed. Bruce King. London: Evans, 1971.

Priebe, Richard. "Fate and Divine Justice in *Things Fall Apart*," *Neo-African Literature and Culture: Essays in Memory of Janheinzjahn*, eds. Lindfors and Ulla Schild. Wiesboden: Mainzer Afrika Studien 1 B. Heymnn, 1976, 159-66.

Ranga Rao, V. "The Hero in Ngugi wa Thiong'o," *Indian Readings in Common-wealth Literature*, ed. G.S. Amur, et al. New Delhi: Sterling, 1985, 132-36.

Ratcliffe, Michael. "Africa Begins: Amos Tutuola, Chinua Achebe," *The Novel Today*. London: Longmans for the British Council, 1968, 28-31.

Ravenscroft, Arthur. *Chinua Achebe*. Harlow: Longmans, 1969.

Robson, C.B. *Ngugi wa Thiong'o*. London: Macmillan, 1979.

Serumaga, Robert. "A Mirror of Integration: Chinua Achebe and James Ngugi," *Protest and Conflict in African Literature*, ed. Cosmo Pieterse and Donald Munro. New York: Africana Publishing Corp., 1969, 70-80.

Sorrenson, M.P.K. *Land Reforms in Kikuyu Country*. Nairobi: Oxford University Press, 1967.

Tibble, Anne, ed. "Chinua Achebe," *African-English Literature: A Short Survey and Anthology of Prose and Poetry upto 1965*. New York: October House, 1965, 101-11.

Viney, A.J. *The Writer and the Past*. M.A. Thesis, University of Kent at Canterbury, 1985.

Walsh, William. "Chinua Achebe," *A Manifold Voice: Studies in Commonwealth Literature*. London: Chatto and Windus, 1970, 48-61.

Wanjala, Chris L. "Achebe: Teacher and Satirist," *Stand-Points in African Literature: A Critical Anthology*, ed. Chris Wanjala, Nairobi, Kampala, Dar es Salaam: East African Literature Bureau, 1973, 161-71.

Wastberg, Per, ed. *The Writer in Modern Africa*. New York: African Publication Corporation, 1969.

Wauthier, C. *The Literature and Thought of Modern Africa*, trans. Shirely Kay. London: Heinemann, 1978.

Were, Gideon S. and Derek A. Wilson. *East Africa through a Thousand Years*. London: 1972.

Wilson, Richard., ed. *Chinua Achebe: Miscellaneous Papers*. Evaston: Northwestern Univ. Program of African Studies, 1970.

Wren, R.M. *Achebe's World: The Historical and Cultural Context of the Novels of Chinua Achebe*. London: Longman, 1980.

Zehersten, Arne. "Ngugi wa Thiong'o: The Mubenzi Tribesman," *East African Literature*. London: Longman, 1983, 82-86.

B. ARTICLES

Aborisade, P.A. "National and Revolutionary Consciousness: Two Phases of Ngugi's Artistic Praxis," *UFAHAMU*, XVIII, 2 (1990), 59-74.

Acworth, Will. "Interview with Ngugi wa Thiong'o, *UFAHAMU*, XVIII, 2 (1990), 41-46.

Ackley, Donald. "The Male-Female Motif in *Things Fall Apart*," *Studies in Black Literature*, V, 1 (1990), 1-6.

Adebayo, Tunji, "The Past and the Present in Chinua Achebe's Novels," *Ife African Studies*, 1 (1974), 66-84.

___. "The Writer and the African Present: Achebe's Crusade against Cynicism and Apathy," *African Studies Association of the West Indies Bulletin*, 7 (1974), 3-16.

Angogo, R. "Achebe and the English Language," *Busara*, 7, ii (1975), 1-14.

Anozie, Sunday O. "The Problem of Communication in Two West African Novels," *Conch*, II, 1 (1970), 12-20.

Ascherson, Neil. "Betrayal: *Anthills of the Savannah*," *New York Review of Books*, 3 (March 1988), 3-4.

Balogun, F. "Ngugi's *Petals of Blood*: A Novel of the People," *Ba Shiru*, X, 2 (n.d), 49-57.

Baloguh, F. Odun. "Ngugi's *Devil on the Cross*: The Novel as Hagiography of a Marxist," *UFAHAMU*, XVI, 2 (1988), 76-92.

Berger, Roger A. "Ngugi's Comic Vision," *Research in African Literature*, XX, 1 (1989), 1-25.

Babilola, E.A. "A Reconsideration of Achebe's *No Longer at Ease*," *Phylon*, 47 (1986), 139-47.

Balogun, F. Odun. "Achebe's 'The Madman': A Poetic Realization of Irony," *Okike*, 23 (1983), 72-79.

Boafo, Y.S. Kantanka. "*Arrow of God*: A Case Study Megalomania," *Asemka*, I, 2 (1974), 16-24.

___. "Okonkwo or the Trimuph of Masculinity as Determinant of the Fall of a Hero,"

Asemka, I, 1 (1974), 7-15.

Bottcher, Karl H. "The Narrative Technique in Achebe's Novels," *Journal of the New African Literature and the Arts*, 13/14 (1972), 1-2.

Brown, H.R. "Igbo Words for the Non-Igbo: Achebe's Artistry in *Arrow of God*," *Research in African Literatures*, 12 (Spring 1981), 69-85.

Brown, L.W. "Cultural Norms and Modes of Perception in Achebe's Fiction," *Research in African Literatures*, III (1972), 21-35.

Brown, Raymond. "Aspects of *Things Fall Apart*," *Mambo Review of Contemporary African Literature* (Salisbury), 1 (November 1974), 11-13.

Butts, Dennis. "The Novels of Chinua Achebe," *Stand*, VIII, 4 (1967), 62-68.

Champion, Ernest A. "The Story of a Man and His People: Chinua Achebe's *Things Fall Apart*," *Negro American Literature Forum*, 8 (1974), 272-77.

Chukwukere, B. Ibe. "That Wet-eared New Graduate . . . " *Transition*, 23 (1965), 7-8.

Cochrane, Judith. "Women as Guardians of the Tribe in Ngugi's Novels," *ACLALS Bulletin*, IV, 5 (1977), 1-11.

Curtis, Lisa. "The Divergence of Art and Ideology in the Later Novels of Ngugi wa Thiong'o: A Critque," *UFAHAMU*, XIII, 2-3 (1984), 186-214.

Drame, Kandioura. "Social Function of Myth and Epic: Mongo Beti and Ngugi wa Thiong'o," *UFAHAMU*, XII, 2 (1983), 44-68.

Dale, James. "Chinua Achebe, Nigerian Novelist," *Queen's Quarterly*, 75 (1968), 460-75.

Dedenuola, J. "The Structure of Achebe's *Things Fall Apart*," *Nigeria Magazine*, 103 (1969-70), 638-39.

DeMott, Benjamin. "Oyiemuno." *American Scholar*, 32 (1963), 292-306.

Egudu, R.N. "Achebe and the Igbo Narrative Tradition," *Research in African Literatures*, 12 (Spring 1981), 43-54.

Ekaney, Nkwelle. "Corruption and Politics in Chinua Achebe's *A Man of the People: An Assessment*," *Presence Africaine*, 104 (1977), 114-26.

Eko, Ebele. "Chinua Achebe and his Critics: Reception of his Novels in English and American Reviews," *Studies in Black Literature*, VI, 3 (1975), 14-20.

Ekwem, B.C. "The Offended 'Chi' in Achebe's Novels—A Reply," *Horizon*, III, 3 (1965), 34-36.

Elders, Derek. "Review of Ngugi's *A Grain of Wheat*" in Elder D. Jones, ed., *African Literature Today*, no. 1, London: Heinemann (1968).

Emenyonu, Ben. "The Battle for Cultural Freedom" in *African Literature and the Arts*, V, 3 (1973).

Eyoh, Hansel Nolumbe. "Ngugi wa Thiong'o," *The Journal of Commonwealth Literature*, XXI, 1 (1986), 162-66.

Ferris, William R. Jr. "Folklore and the African Novelist: Achebe and Tutuola," *Journal of American Folklore*, 86 (1973), 25-36.

Gere, Anne Ruggles. "An Approach to Achebe's Fiction," *Africa Quarterly* (New Delhi), XVI, 2 (1976), 27-35.

Green, Robert. "Nigeria's New Man," *Nation*, 19 (April 1966), 465-66.

Goodwin, K.L. "Nationality-Chauvinism Must Burn. Utopian Visions in *Petals of Blood* and *Matigari*," *The Literary Criterion*, XXVII, 3 (1991), 1-14.

Gordimer, Nadine. "A Tyranny of Clowns," *New York Times Book Review*, 21 (Feburary 1988), 1 & 26.

Gowdah, H.H. "The Novels of Chinua Achebe," *Literary Half-Yearly*, XIV, 2 (1973), 3-9.

Griffiths, G. "Language and Action in the Novels of Chinua Achebe," *African Literature Today*, V (1971), 88-105.

Harrow, Kenneth. "Ngugi wa Thiong'o's *A Grain of Wheat:* Season of Irony," *Research in African Literatures*, XVI, 2 (1985), 243-63.

Heywood, Christopher. "Surface and Symbol in *Things Fall Apart*," *Journal of the Nigerian*

English Studies Association, 2 (1967), 41-45.

Ige, Seun. "*Morning Yet on Creation Day*," *Afriscope*, V, 10 (1975), 33-36.

Ike, Rosaline, "Tragedy and Social Purpose: The Novels of Chinua Achebe," *Something*, 5 (1966), 3-13.

Ikiddeh, Ime. "James Ngugi as Novelist," *African Literature Today*, 2 (1969), 3-10.

Indrasena Reddy, K. "Optimism in Ngugi's *Petals of Blood*," *Kakatiya Journal of English Studies*, 8 (1987-88), 134-43.

Innes, C.L. "A Source for *Arrow of God*," *Research in African Literatures*, 9 (1978), 16-18.

Iyasere, Solomon. "Narrative Techniques in *Things Fall Apart*," *New Letters*, 40 (1974), 73-93.

Jabbi, Bu-Buakei. "Myth and Ritual in *Arrow of God*," *African Literature Today*, XI (1980), 130-48.

___. "Fire and Transition in *Things Fall Apart*," *Obsidian*, I, 3 (1975), 22-36.

___. "Conrad's Influence on Betrayal in *A Grain of Wheat*," *Research in African Literatures*, XI, 1 (Spring 1980), 50-83.

___. "The Structure of Symbolism in *A Grain of Wheat*," *Research in African Literatures*, XVI, 2 (1985), 210-42.

Jervis, Stephen. "Tradition and Change in Hardy and Achebe," *Black Orpheus*, II, 5-6 (1971), 31-38.

Johnson, John W. "Folklore in Achebe's Novels," *New Letters*, vol. 40, no. 3 (1974), 95-107.

Jones, Eldred. "Language and Theme in *Things Fall Apart*." *Review of English Literature*, V, 4 (1964), 39-43.

Jordan, John O. "Culture Conflict and Social Change in Achebe's *Arrow of God*," *Critique*, XIII, 1 (1971), 66-82.

Kemoli, A.M. "The Novels of Chinua Achebe: A Prophecy of Violence," *Joliso*, II, 1 (1974), 47-66.

Klima, Vladimir. "Chinua Achebe's Novels," *Philologica Pragensia*, 12 (1969), 32-34.

King, B.A. "The Revised *Arrow of God*," *African Literature Today*, XIII (1983), 69-78.

Kronenfeld, J.Z. "The 'Communalistic' African and the 'Individualistic' Westerner: Some Comments on Misleading Generalizations in Western Criticism of Soyinka and Achebe," *Research in African Literatures*, VI (1975), 199-225.

Kuesgen, Reinhardt. "Conrad and Achebe: Aspects of the Novel," *WLWE*, vol. 24 (Summer 1984), 27-33.

Kozain, Rustom, "From as Politics, or the Tyranny of Narrativity. Rereading Ngugi wa Thiong'o's *Petals of Blood*," *UFAHAMU*, XVIII, 3 (1990), 77-90.

Landrum, Roger. "Chinua Achebe and the Aristotelian Concept of Tragedy," *Black Academy Review*, I, 1 (1970), 22-30.

Leach, Josephine. "A Study of Chinua Achebe's *Things Fall Apart* in Mid America," *English Journal*, 60 (1971), 1052-56.

Leslie, Omolara. "Chinua Achebe: His Vision and His Craft," *Black Orpheus*, II, 7 (1972), 34-41.

___. "Nigeria, Alienation and the Novels of Achebe," *Presence Africaine*, (1972), 99-108.

Lewis, Mary Ellen B. "Beyond Content in the Analysis of Folklore in Literature: Chinua Achebe's *Arrow of God*," *Research in African Literatures*, VII (1976), 44-52.

Lewis, Maureen W. "Ezeulu and his God: An Analysis of *Arrow of God*," *Black World*, XXIV, 2 (1974), 71-87.

___. "Priest of a Dead God," *African Studies Association of the West Indies Bulletin*, 7 (1974), 39-53.

Lindfors, Bernth. "The Palm Oil with which Achebe's Words are Eaten," *African Literature Today*, 1 (1968), 3-18.

___. "Achebe's African Parable," *Presence Africaine*, 66 (1968), 130-36.

___. "The Folktale as Paradigm in Chinua Achebe's *Arrow of God*," *Studies in Black Litera-*

ture, I, 1 (1970), 1-15.

___. "Chinua Achebe's Proverbs," *Nigerian Field*, 35 (1970), 180-85.

___. "Maxims, Proverbial Phrases, and Other Sententious Sayings in Achebe's Novels," *Nigerian Filed*, 36 (1971), 139-43.

___. "Ambiguity and Intention in *Arrow of God*," *Ba Shiru*, V, 1 (1973), 43-48.

___. "Chinua Achebe," in Frederick Ungar and Lina Mainiero, eds. *Encylopedia of World Literature in the 20th Century*, vol. 4 (1975), 4-7.

___. "The Blind Men and the Elephant," *African Literature Today*, 7 (1975), 53-64.

Macebuh, Stanley. "On the Question of Theme in Nigerian Literature: A Rejoinder to an Address by Chinua Achebe," *Horizon*, III, 4 (1966), 14-16.

Maduka, Chaukwudi. "Irony and Vision in Achebe's *A Man of the People*," *Ba Shiru*, 8, i (1977), 19-30.

Maughan-Brown, David. "Four Sons One Father: A Comparison of Ngugi's Earliest Novels with Works by Mwangi, Mangua, and Wachira," *Research in African Literatures*, XVI, 2 (1985), 179-209.

Mazuri, Alamin and Lupenga, Mhande. "The Historical Imperative in African Activist Literature," *UFAHAMU*, XVII, 2 (1990), 47-58.

McDaniel, Richard B. "The Python Episodes in Achebe's Novels," *International Fiction Review*, 3 (1976), 100-6.

___. "Of What Is Past, Or Passing, or to Come," *Studies in Black Literature*, II, 1 (1971), 9-13.

Melamu, M.J. "The Quest for Power in Achebe's *Arrow of God*," *English Studies in Africa*, XIV (1971), 225-40.

Melone, Thomas. "Architecture du Monde: Chinua Achebe et W.B. Yeats," *Conch*, II, 1 (1970), 44-52.

Meyers, Jeffrey. "Culture and History in *Things Fall Apart*," *Critique*, XI, 1 (1969), 25-32.

Mohan, Devinder. "Semiology of Waringa's Dream in Ngugi's *Devil on the Cross*" in R.K. Dhawan, *Commonwealth Fiction*, 2 (1988), 203-19.

Monkman, Laslie. "Keynya and the New Jerusalem in *A Grain of Wheat*," *African Literature Today*, 7 (1975), 112.

Nance, Carolyn. "Cosmology in the Novels of Chinua Achebe," *Conch*, III, 2 (1971), 121-36.

Nnolim, C.E. "Form and Function of the Folk Tradition in Achebe's Novels," *Ariel*, XIV (1983), 35-47.

"Achebe's *Things Fall Apart*: An Igbo National Epic," *Black Academy Review*, II, 1/2 (1971), 55-60.

"A Source for *Arrow of God*," *Research in African Literature*, VIII (1977), 1-26.

Nwoga, D.I. "The Igbo World of Achebe's *Arrow of God*," *Research in African Literatures*, XII (Spring 1981), 14-42.

___. "The Chi Offended," *Transition*, 15 (1964), 5.

Obilade, Tony. "The Stylistic Function of Pidgin English in African Literature: Achebe and Soyinka," *Research in African Literatures*, 9 (1978), 433-44.

Obiechina, Emmanuel. "Structure and Significance in Achebe's *Things Fall Apart*," *English in Africa*, II, 2 (1975), 39-44.

Ogunbesan, Kolawole. "Politics and the African Writer: The Example of Chinua Achebe," *Work in Progress* (Zaria), 2 (1973), 75-93.

Okafor, Clem A. "The Instructability of the Gods: Motivation of Behaviour in Chinua Achebe's *Arrow of God*," *Presence Africaine*, 63 (1967), 207-14.

Okunnuga Yemi. "The Tragic Conflict in Achebe's *No Longer at Ease*," *Journal of the Nigerian English Studies Association*, 2 (1968), 141-42.

Olney, James. "The African Novel in Transition: Chinua Achebe," *South Atlantic Quarterly*, 70 (1971), 229-316.

Ogu, J.N. "The Concept of Madness in Chinua Achebe's Writings," *Journal of Commonwealth Literature*, XVIII, 1 (1983), 48-54.

Oko, Emilia A. "The Historical Novel of Africa: A Sociological Approach to Achebe's *Things Fall Apart* and *Arrow of God,*" *Conch*, VI, 1/2 (1974), 15-46.

Okpaku, Joseph. "A Novel for the People," *Journal of the New African Literature*, II (Fall 1966), 76-80.

Nkankwo. Chimalum. "Siftingt the grain from the husk: an Overview of Ngugi's writing," *The Literary Half-Yearly*, XXV, 1 (1984), 2-15.

___. "Women in Ngugi's Plays: From Passivity to Social Responsibility," *UFAHAMU*, XIV, 3 (1985), 85-92.

Pagnoulle, Christine, "Ngugi wa Thiong'o's 'Journey of the Magi': part 2 of *Petals of Blood*," *Research in African Literatures*, XVI, 2 (1985), 264-75.

Palmer. E. "Ngugi's Petals of Blood," *ALT*, 10 (1979), 153-66.

Peck, Richard. "Hermits and Saviors, Osagyefos and Healers: Artists and Intellectuals in the Works of Ngugi and Armah," *Research in African Literatures*, XX, 1 (1989), 26-49.

Penfold, Jill. "Chinua Achebe—His Reaction to Change in Nigeria," *Mambo Review of Contemporary African Literature*, 3 (August 1974), 10-11.

Porter, Abioseh M. "Ideology and the Image of Women: Kenyan Woken in Njau and Ngugi," *Ariel*, XII, 3 (July 1981), 61-74.

Ponuthurai, Charles Sarvan. "The Pessimism of Chinua Achebe," *Critique*, XV, 3 (1974), 95-109.

Read, John. "James Ngugi and the African Novel," *JCL*, I, 2 (1965), 117-21.

___. "Ngugi's New Strength," A Review of *A Grain of Wheat, JCL*, 5 (July 1968), 135-36

Riddy, Felicity. "Language as a Theme in *No Longer at Ease*," *Journal of Commonwealth Literature*, IX, (1970), 38-47.

Rogers, Philip. "*No Longer at Ease:* Chinua Achebe's 'Heart of Whiteness'," *Research in African Literatures*, XIV (1983), 164-83.

Scheub, Harold. "When a Man Fails Alone," *Presence Africaine*, vol. 74 (1970), 61-89.

Seitel, Peter, "Proverbs: A Social Use of Metaphor," *Genre*, 2 (1969), 143-61.

Sharma, Govind Narain. "Ngugi's *Detained* as a Modern Consolatio," *Research in African Literatures,* XIX, 4 (1988), 520- 28.

___. "Ngugi's Christian Vision: Theme and Pattern in *A Grain of Wheat*," *African Literature Today*, 10 (1979), 167-76.

___. "Socialism and Civilization: The Revolutionary Traditionalism of Ngugi wa Thiong'o," *Ariel*, XIX, 2 (1988), 21-30.

Sicherman, Carol M. "Ngugi wa Thiong'o and the Writing of Kenyan History," *Research in African Literatures*, XX, 3 (1989), 347-70.

Sivaramakrishnan, V. "James Ngugi," *Triveni*, vol. 55, no. 1 (1986), 28-37.

Shelton, Austin J. "The Offended Chi in Achebe's Novels," *Transition*, 13 (1964), 36-37.

___. "The 'Palm-Oil' of Language: Proverbs in Chinua Achebe's Novels," *Modern Language Quarterly*, 30 (1969), 86-111.

Sibley, Francis M. "Tragedy in the Novels of Chinua Achebe." *Southern Humanities Review*, 9 (1975), 359-73.

Soile, Sola. "Tragic Paradox in Achebe's *Arrow of God*," *University Review*, 37 (1970), 157-58.

Stock, A.G. "Yeats and Achebe," *Journal of Commonwealth Literature*, V (1968), 105-11.

Swados, Harvey. "Chinua Achebe and the Writers of Biafra," *Sarah Lawrence Journal* (Spring 1970), 55-62.

Taiwo, Oladele. "Successful Essays," *Home Studies*, 36 (1967), 23-24.

Turkington, Kate. "This no be them country: Chinua Achebe's Novels," *English Studies in Africa*, 14 (1971), 205-14.

Udmukwu, Onyemaechi. "Achebe and the Negation of Independence," *Modern Fiction*

Studies, vol. 37, 3 (Antumn 1991).

Unezinwa, Willy A. "The Idiom of Plastic Figures in Chinua Achebe's Novels," *NSAL*, 3 (October 1980), 13-21.

Urs, S.N. Vikamraj. "*Things Fall Apart*: A Novel from the 'Dark' Continent," *Commonwealth Quarterly*, I, 1 (1976), 28-34.

Vincent, Theo. "Register in Achebe," *Journal of the Nigerian English Studies Association*, VI, 1 (1974), 95-106.

___. "The Post-war Achebe," *Nigeria Magazine*, 113 (1974), 95-106.

Wali, Obiajunwa. "The Dead End of African Literature," *Transition*, III, 10 (1963).

Weinstock, Donald and Cathy Ramadan. "Symbolic Structure in *Things Fall Apart*," *Critique*, XI, 1 (1969), 33-41.

Weinstock, Donald J. "Achebe's Christ-Figure," *Journal of the New African Literature and the Arts*, 5/6 (1968), 20-26.

___. "The Two Swarms of Locusts: Judgement by Indirection in *Things Fall Apart*," *Studies in Black Literature*, II, 1 (1971), 14-19.

Williams, Lloyd. "Religion and Life in James Ngugi's *The River Between*," *African Literature Today*, 5 (1971), 54-65.

Wilson, Roderick. "Eliot and Achebe: An Analysis of Some Formal and Philosophic Qualities of *No Longer at Ease*," *English Studies in Africa*, 14 (1971), 215-23.

Wren Robert M. "Anticipations of Civil Conflict in Nigerian Novels: Aluko and Achebe," *Studies in Black Literature*, II, 1 (1970), 21-32.

___. "*Arrow of God*," *Afriscope*, IX, 5 (1975), 43-44.

___. "Achebe's Revisions of *Arrow of God*," *Research in African Literatures*, 7 (1976), 53-58.

___. "From Ulu to Christ: The Transfer of Faith in *Arrow of God*," *Christianity and Literature*, XXVII, 2 (1978), 28-40.

___. "Race and Duality: Achebe in the Morning," *Afriscope*, VI, 4 (1976), 31-32.

Wynter, Sylvia. "History, Ideology and the Reinvention of the Past in Achebe's *Things Fall Apart* and Laye's *The Dark Child*," *Minority Voices*, II, 1 (1978), 43-61.

Yankson, Kofi. "The Use of Pidgin in *No Longer at Ease* and *A Man of the People*," *Asemka*, I, 2 (1974), 68-79.

Zehersten, Arne. "Ngugi wa Thiong'o: The Mubenzi Tribesman," *East African Literature*, London: Longman (1983), 82-86.

Index